TINY KEEPER
STEVE DEATH

TINY KEEPER
STEVE DEATH

Record Breaker, Shy Genius and Maverick

Alan Hester

First published by Pitch Publishing, 2025

1

Pitch Publishing
9 Donnington Park,
85 Birdham Road,
Chichester, West Sussex,
PO20 7AJ
www.pitchpublishing.co.uk
info@pitchpublishing.co.uk

© 2025, Alan Hester

Every effort has been made to trace the copyright.
Any oversight will be rectified in future editions at the
earliest opportunity by the publisher.

All rights reserved. No part of this book may be reproduced, sold or utilised in any form or transmitted in any form or by any means, electronic or mechanical, including photocopying, recording or by any information storage and retrieval system, without prior permission in writing from the publisher.

A CIP catalogue record is available for this book
from the British Library.

ISBN 978 1 80150 951 0

Typesetting and origination by Pitch Publishing

Printed and bound on FSC® certified paper in line with
our continuing commitment to ethical business practices,
sustainability and the environment.

Printed and bound in India by Thomson Press

Contents

Foreword by David Downs 9

Author's Introduction 14

Prologue: The End of the Beginning 17

1. West Ham United and the Academy of Football 24
2. The Legend Begins – in the Third Division 49
3. Life in the Basement 67
4. A Load of Old Bull .105
5. 1,103 Minutes 127
6. Testimonial Season .160
7. The Beginning of the End 181
8. The Fans' Perspective 202
9. The End, and Final Thoughts 228

Acknowledgements 243

The Making of *Tiny Keeper* 251

Appendix 254

For Kathy and Shirley

And with thanks to Richard Wickson and Alan Bunce

Foreword by David Downs

OCCASIONALLY IN our lives we are lucky enough to meet someone we will remember for one of two special reasons. Either they possess some outstanding skill which we can only observe and admire, or they have a depth of character which will leave a lasting impression on us.

Such a person was Steve Death, or 'Deathy' as he was known to his team-mates at Reading Football Club, where he was the first-choice goalkeeper between 1969 and 1982. Alan Hester's biography of Steve tells us in forensic detail of the life of a talented young footballer who began his career as a speedy winger, then was converted to a brave and acrobatic goalkeeper with such success that he was selected for the England Schoolboys under-15 team, played one game in the First Division for West Ham United, then stood between the posts for Reading for more than 500 matches.

Along the way he had to show his resilience and courage by overcoming some injuries which might have deterred a lesser person, including playing throughout a game at Huddersfield despite suffering from a broken jaw, but volunteering to do so because the only other available goalie was struggling with an even more serious injury. But he had his stubborn streak too as the story shows, once needing to be hauled out of bed on a Saturday morning to play at Gillingham, having originally refused to do so due to a dispute over wages.

Much colour is added to the text through interviews with former players, at West Ham and Reading, who have memories of Steve and can give a professional assessment of his goalkeeping style as well as his character. And there are contributions from Reading supporters who watched him during his career at Elm Park and were keen to pay their own tribute to a person who almost literally held their hopes and ambitions in his hands for more than a decade of Saturday afternoons. Especially interesting in this latter collection of tributes is a poem written by a young female supporter, and an analysis of Steve's goalkeeping technique – especially his kicking – by former senior amateur goalkeeper Pete Glanville, lately a goalkeeping coach at York City.

It is worth pointing out at this stage that one of the most generous tributes came from John Turner, an aspiring young goalie who had to be content with reserve-team football for so long due to Steve's consistency. The 'goalkeepers' union' is also represented by Alan Hester and myself; Alan would fill in as emergency cover for his teams, while I played for some time as a regular goalkeeper.

So we have both stood between the posts on a Saturday afternoon or Sunday morning trying to emulate, without much success, the ability shown by Steve.

It is a truism that all good things must inevitably come to an end and the final season at Elm Park for Steve was 1981/82. He had been replaced as first-choice goalkeeper by Ron Fearon and was restricted to just three appearances. After his final match, on 17 February 1982, he walked away from football. His frustration was compounded by the need to move his family out of the club house in Tilehurst Road, and they all moved back for a while to Elmswell in his native Suffolk, where Steve was persuaded to play a handful of games as goalkeeper for the local village team.

By now, however, he had outgrown the sedate country lifestyle and we can read how the comparative buzz of the big town brought the family back to Reading, where some of the contacts he had made as a much admired sportsman enabled him to get a job as a greenkeeper at the nearby Mapledurham Golf Club. By coincidence the vice-captain at Mapledurham was Colin Gunney, who had, as a local sports journalist, reported on many of the matches in which Steve had played and had also taken the initiative in leading his testimonial committee. Steve and Colin chatted occasionally, more frequently about the golf course than about football. But the quiet life of a greenkeeper was an admirable fit for Steve as he could spend as much time as he wanted working quietly on his own, no doubt reflecting occasionally on the times when he had been the object of scrutiny by thousands of spectators.

Steve's peaceful and enjoyable lifestyle was shattered when he became ill, was diagnosed with cancer and had to stop working. He was admitted to the Duchess of Kent Hospice in Liebenrood Road, little more than a goal kick away from the Elm Park ground, the scene of so many of his triumphs. He fought the illness with the same courage he had shown when diving among the lunging bodies and muddy boots of so many hectic Saturday afternoons and midweek evenings.

Steve's death at the age of just 54 was a terrible tragedy, primarily for his family of course, but also for those of us who had seen him play. Many of his former team-mates as well as supporters attended his humanist funeral at Henley Road crematorium, where Colin and I had been asked by Sharon, Steve's partner, to give the address and pay tribute to his many achievements. It was a privilege for us both to do so.

It is rare to find such a detailed account of a footballer's career and lifestyle, especially of one whose time was spent playing in the lower divisions of the Football League, where a professional's existence could be far from glamorous. But this fascinating biography does exactly that and we should be grateful to the author for his diligence. Most of all, however, we should acknowledge the opportunity to have watched the best goalkeeper in the history of Reading Football Club. Thanks for the memories, Steve.

David Downs

Reading FC club historian

Author's Introduction

THIS BOOK is about a genuine hero, with contributions from other heroes, most of whom remain unknown to the wider world. If it's been written to pay homage to them, it has also been written for my tribe. Writing it has reconnected me with them and brought back so many emotions I'd almost forgotten, and has changed and charged them again, as time always will. I hope reading it does the same for you, regardless of who you support.

It may only be football, and I know it may not seem important in the great scheme of things. Not only is it *only* football, but it's *lower-league* football. Far from the multi-million-pound industry of today, this was football played against a backdrop of uncompromising concrete terraces and iron crush barriers, often with empty spaces between the scattered groups of spectators.

Its stars lived locally among the fans, drank in the same pubs, took their children to the same schools and chatted to supporters in the club bar after games. Their deeds were reported in the local paper and commentary was carried at best by local hospital radio, where I remember hearing the late, great Robin Friday score two goals on debut against Exeter City while I was waiting for a small operation.

Steve Death was in that team, as he was nearly every week for 13 years, achieving things that seemed magical to me, pulling off saves he had no right to make, and each goal scored against him became an insult to the natural order of things. In reality in the early days it was an insult we had to get used to, as Steve came into a team midway through a season in which our cavalier style of play saw us concede 77 goals while scoring 87, but he put that right by the end of the decade by breaking the record for the longest time in Football League history without conceding a single goal.

Beyond the statistics, this tiny goalkeeper, at 5ft 7.5in the smallest in all four divisions, made an instant impact and became a club legend. On his debut the local paper described him as 'an insignificantly built bundle of daredevil energy' and he was voted as the club's player of the year four times – the first when he was still on loan from First Division West Ham United and officially not a Reading player.

There were plenty of cold, damp evenings at the old Elm Park watching goalless draws against other unfashionable teams, and plenty of long away trips to watch rank bad performances, but in ways that perhaps only a lower-league supporter can understand, that was always the point. For a few thousand of us, who lived off a regular sprinkling of Third or Fourth Division stardust, as Bill Shankly almost said, football really was a matter of life and Death.

   With best wishes,

   Alan

Prologue

The End of the Beginning

Manchester City: Dowd, Book, Pardoe, Doyle, Booth, Oakes, Summerbee, Bell, Lee, Young, Coleman

West Ham United: Death, Moore, Stephenson, Bonds, Lampard, Boyce, Brooking, Peters, Sissons, Hurst, Redknapp

When the young Stephen Death ran out for West Ham United at Maine Road to play Manchester City in April 1969, he was part of a team containing some of the greatest players to ever play the game. Geoff Hurst, Bobby Moore and Martin Peters had been part of England's legendary 1966 World Cup-winning side; other stars such as Harry Redknapp, Frank Lampard, Trevor Brooking, Billy Bonds and John Sissons were also in the Hammers' team for a 1-1 draw against the previous season's First Division champions.

City had Mike Summerbee, Colin Bell and Francis Lee – their own trio of club legends. They also had other greats such as Tony Book, Neil Young and Glyn Pardoe, whose

71st-minute shot came off the post to become the solitary goal Death was to concede at the highest level of English football. The Citizens had won the FA Cup four days before the match, beating Leicester City 1-0, and paraded the trophy to their fans moments before kick-off. This was the pinnacle of the game, and Steve was sharing a pitch with the top players of the day, in the top division of the English Football League.

There was only ever one thing that prevented Steve from being a regular for West Ham as their number one goalkeeper, or from moving on to another top-flight club. This was the same thing that in the opinion of everyone who saw him play also stopped him from playing for England. His height.

At 5ft 7.5in he was considered too small to be a top-class goalkeeper, but according to every professional who ever played with him, he had every other attribute to be the very best. Skill, bravery, positional sense, speed and for a quiet man, the ability to dominate his area and as one centre-half says, to loudly and clearly 'let you know'. Harry Redknapp saw him in training every day and describes him as 'an incredible goalkeeper, a great, great goalkeeper'. Dave Llewellyn, a striker who played in the youth team with him at West Ham, calls him 'the best young goalkeeper I have ever seen'. Stuart Morgan, another team-mate, both at West Ham and later at Reading, describes him as 'a different class'.

Llewellyn says now, 'If Steve had been my height he would have played for England.' Llewellyn was 6ft 1in. The difference between international stardom and a career in the Third and Fourth Divisions was just six inches.

Death was kept out of the first team by regulars Bobby Ferguson and Peter Grotier, and there was little future at West Ham as a third-choice goalkeeper. Although he would have more brushes with greatness in the next few years, this was the closest he would get to the status his talent deserved.

As football debuts go, it doesn't get much better. That day's crowd of 31,846 would be the biggest he ever played in front of as a professional, and he saw a Martin Peters header give his team the lead before being pegged back by Pardoe's late goal. It could have led to a glittering career at the top echelons of the game, but it didn't, and everyone knew it.

A newspaper strike meant there were no Sunday papers to record the game for posterity, and the match report on the following Monday in the *Manchester Guardian* didn't even mention his name, showing Ferguson's name on the team sheet, as did the matchday programme.

In reality, this was a relaxed, end-of-season game with nothing riding on it for either side and by November the following season he had left Upton Park, going on loan to Third Division Reading in search of first-team football.

He made such an impression there that the move was made permanent as soon as Reading could afford the transfer fee of £20,000 – the highest they had paid in their entire history at that time. It took the Royals until the beginning of the following season to raise the money and for an unfashionable club with a parsimonious board of directors and few previous signs of ambition this was a huge vote of confidence in their tiny keeper.

Death may have missed out on the big time, but in moving to Reading he became a club legend and a hero to many, breaking local and national records and playing 537 first-team games over a 13-year career. In his time at Reading, Death was voted player of the year four times, with the first award coming while still on loan from West Ham while the board scrambled to find the money to sign him. He was also selected twice by his fellow professionals for the PFA's divisional team of the year.

Far from being a disappointment, this move was the start of a truly special career.

Playing with Death

Stuart Morgan (West Ham, 1967-69; Reading, 1969-72)

A former Welsh amateur boxing champion, centre-half Morgan joined West Ham as a teenager in 1967, and following a loan spell with Torquay United he eventually moved to Reading with Death in 1969, signing on the same day. He made 48 appearances for the club before moving on to successful spells at Colchester United and AFC Bournemouth. When his playing career ended he went into management with Weymouth, Torquay United and Dorchester Town before working in scouting for his former West Ham colleague Harry Redknapp back at Bournemouth.

He was a bit of a loner. Loud enough on the pitch but off it he kept himself to himself. He went home at weekends a lot more than most players. He wasn't quiet on the pitch at all. Between him and Dave Llewellyn their friendship and support kept me at West Ham when I was a teenager missing my family back in Wales.

Steve and I couldn't have picked a much tougher baptism to our professional football careers than the East End of London during the late 60s and with a top First Division club, renowned for its coaching abilities with Ron Greenwood the head of coaching and management. I left home on the beautiful Gower coastline in south-west Wales at 17 years and Steve had come from a very close family in rural Norton, in beautiful Suffolk. Along with another Welsh signing, Dave Llewellyn from Penarth, we were all in the same boat of being terribly homesick, but we all became great comrades who helped one another at lonely times with our digs nearby.

None of ours turned out to be glamorous careers with Steve and I joining Reading and Dave signing for Peterborough in the lower divisions, but we all played numerous Football League games, which we all can be proud of.

Steve's enthusiasm for coaching and management was low, which sadly saw him drift away from the game and friends he knew well, which was such a sad end for such a popular goalkeeper.

Dave Llewellyn (West Ham 1969-71)

Llewellyn was close to both Death and Morgan, living in nearby digs and playing in the same youth and reserve teams. The centre-forward made six appearances for the first team at West Ham before moving to Peterborough United, scoring 15 times in 63 appearances.

I got transferred to Peterborough and I scored against him when we played Reading, and he absolutely hated it. He was the nicest person you could ever wish to meet, but he could have made it as a top pro. He would have made the England team without a doubt. He was a good friend. He went on loan and signed for Reading. If you saw him he would always have a nice talk with you – and a cigarette!

He turned down the England youth team when we were at West Ham. He didn't give a reason; he just didn't want to do it. When he played for England Schoolboys, he kept Peter Shilton out of the side. If Steve had grown taller, Shilton wouldn't have got a game, he was that good.

1

West Ham United and the Academy of Football

Football and friendship at 'the club that won the World Cup'

STEVE DEATH was born in Norton, in the Suffolk countryside, the son of Peter and Margery Death, and the family moved to Elmswell when he was still a toddler. The village was extremely remote, miles from the nearest town or settlement, and life in this deeply rural setting gave the young boy a lifelong love of the natural world – an environment he would return to after football in his eventual home in Berkshire.

Death was firmly rooted in the countryside and came from a long line of agricultural workers and artisans with farm labourers, stockmen, carpenters, gardeners and millers among the trades of his grandparents and great-grandparents. These were hard jobs, physically demanding and low-paid, and involved a lifetime of commitment, working outside in all weathers to earn enough to feed their families. The outdoor life and the natural world were in his veins. Interestingly, his maternal grandfather Samuel Brinkley, another labourer, was just 5ft 5in tall, so it would seem his genes were to have a major influence on his grandson's future.

A famously quiet and reserved man, Death was never someone who welcomed authority of any kind, and he saw football as a perfect way to escape the disciplines of school, which he found irrelevant and irksome. An intelligent but unconventional boy, he loved the freedom the game gave him, allowing him to focus on something outside of himself and express himself through physical movement and common endeavour.

He stumbled on goalkeeping by accident, having started his football career as a promising right-winger as part of the under-12 team at Beyton Modern School near Bury St Edmunds. He was quick and slightly built, and right wing was an obvious position for him until he injured a knee while practising crosses one afternoon in training. He went in goal for the rest of the session and did so well there that he took over the position; from that moment on he never played anywhere else again.

Goalkeeping was the perfect fit for a boy who preferred to be an individual, alone with his own thoughts and priorities, and not restricted by anyone else's rules. The skills he needed could be thought about and honed without adherence to too much collective coaching and without the drills everyone else had to undergo. He could be an integral part of a team but separate from them too, making a vital contribution but making it in his own way.

In the 1962/63 season, at the age of 13 he was a regular in the school's first team and was chosen by the district team, West Suffolk, to play for the under-15 representative side against a German touring side. He got his first rave reviews after that game, with the *Bury Free Press* writing, 'Hero of the match was the youngest player in the West Suffolk side, 13-year-old goalkeeper Stephen Death.'

His lack of interest in formality of any kind was to be a mixed blessing throughout his career, but his natural talent and determination got him noticed from a young age, with scouts from several clubs watching him and giving their employers positive reports. At the same time, he appeared unaffected by their attention, his ambitions extending mainly to continuing to play football as a much better alternative to going to school and studying for exams.

Death's rise was little short of meteoric, playing above his age group in representative teams and moving up to the Suffolk county side. It wasn't long before people started taking notice as he rose through the representative ranks, at first locally and then nationally. In 1964/65 he gave what was reported as a 'marvellous display of goalkeeping' to help Suffolk win the Home Counties Championship London Cup, beating Kent 2-1 at Gillingham FC's ground for his county's first triumph in the competition. He was noticed by a host of professional clubs including Arsenal, Portsmouth, Ipswich Town and Watford, and spent a week on trial at Tottenham Hotspur. Things were hotting up.

Next up was an invitation to join a coaching course at Bisham Abbey and after various trials he was called up to the full England Schoolboys squad in 1965, raising his profile further by making three appearances for them and gaining rave reviews. His debut came against Wales at Sheffield Wednesday's Hillsborough ground. The *FA Year Book*'s verdict was, 'Stephen Death, playing his first game in goal for England, fully justified his selection with some daring saves.' He kept a clean sheet in a 0-0 draw in that first game and kept two more in the next two, a 3-0 victory against West Germany and a 2-0 win in the return against Wales at Ninian Park. Playing internationally gave him a wealth of experiences, travelling and playing with the cream of the country's young players and exposing him to coaching and scrutiny from some senior and respected figures in the game.

Among the other players in the group was his rival for the goalkeeper's jersey – a certain Peter Shilton. Many good judges felt that Death was Shilton's equal in terms of talent, agility and positional awareness, and forecast a great future for the young lad. A crucial difference between them, however, was their physical stature. Shilton was already growing into the ideal goalkeeper's physique: tall, strong and muscular.

While Shilton kept developing physically, Death did not, never growing beyond his eventual 5ft 7.5in and remaining slim and small in stature.

There was another difference, too. While Shilton famously continued to work on his physical strength and stature by, among other things, hanging from the bannisters at his parents' home in an effort to add a bit more height, Death was characteristically uninterested in discipline and disinclined to perform any unnecessary activity.

Many years later, Shilton reflected on their time together in Death's testimonial match programme, 'I can remember playing for England Schoolboys against Scotland at Wembley in front of an 80,000 crowd and looking forward to playing in the Olympic Stadium in Berlin against West Germany in our next match. However, Steve was picked for this game which was played in front of 75,000 people. I envied him.

'In 1965 we shared the England Schoolboys goalkeeper's jersey. You could say that the competition between the two of us in those days could be compared to the competition I experience today with Ray Clemence.'

Shilton went on to win league titles and European Cups, play in World Cups and become England's most-capped player with 125 appearances over 20 years. Death, as ever, took his own very different path.

One notable early show of interest in England Schoolboys' tiny keeper came from perhaps the greatest and most romantic club in the land at the time. Manchester United, with its proud and of course tragic history of putting their faith in youngsters and growing some of the outstanding players of the time, invited him for trials. Steve turned them down. He was very close to his family, in particular his mum, and felt that moving from Suffolk to Manchester as a 15-year-old was too big a sacrifice to make.

How many boys would reject an opportunity like that? It didn't matter to him what other people might say, or what conventional wisdom decided about anything. As with so many situations later in life, he did what he wanted to do, regardless of what others might have thought or advised. He was his own man, and having decided what he thought was right for him, that was that.

However, when in 1965 West Ham came and asked the brilliant young goalkeeper to leave his family and his beloved rural Suffolk home to come to London, he said yes.

The East End

As exciting as it was to be starting a career as a professional footballer, swapping the heart of the Suffolk countryside for the crowded and closely built terraced streets of London was a huge challenge. Steve was away from his family and everyone and everything he had known all his life. He was still a teenager, at an age when most boys would still be at school, and just starting to think about their future life.

For an apprentice footballer, this was the norm. Boys and young men across the land were leaving their families to try their luck in the harshest, most competitive of environments and with the odds of making the grade incredibly slim.

It was common for promising young players to get so close to their goal they could smell it, only to be told at the age of 19 or 20 that they were being let go, with the difference between the realisation of their dreams and a shattering dose of reality being wafer thin. Careers were made or broken on the judgement of a manager about ability or character, or that cruellest of occupational hazards: injury. Rejection could mean being left without a trade or an education and having to fend for themselves in the adult world with their dreams in tatters.

On the other hand, those dreams were so bright they were worth the risk and couldn't be fulfilled in any other way. Those unfavourable odds would be far away from their thoughts when they were starting out, plucked from their local leagues and representative teams because they were seen as having something special. In the beginning, everyone is going to make it. Why else would they be there?

The friendships made in this situation meant everything. On arrival from the Suffolk countryside, Death moved into digs a short walk from Upton Park. There he met fellow youth player Dave Llewellyn and, later, Stuart Morgan; all of them still in their teens and away from home and family for the first time, needing to settle quickly in order to survive and adapt to a whole new way of life.

Stuart and Steve lived 'a hop, skip and jump' across the road from each other and Dave next door to Steve. On the day Morgan arrived he left his digs and saw a young chap coming out of the house opposite, so asked, 'Excuse me, if you don't mind me asking, are you anything to do with West Ham?' 'Yes,' said the young man, 'I'm an apprentice goalkeeper.' 'I've been here about two minutes,' said Morgan, 'I've just arrived from Swansea.' The two met and became friends before they had even trained together and in Morgan's words, were 'a great help to each other then, and all the way through the next three seasons'. Llewellyn echoes these sentiments, saying, 'We were such a good team together. Every Saturday and on a Wednesday night we would go for a drink, and we just walked everywhere. We looked after each other. I thought the world of him.'

Morgan still remembers how hard it was for a bunch of young men arriving in the East End 'with the Krays walking about'. With everything they knew taken away from them, staying with kind but unfamiliar people in someone else's home, the three formed a band of brothers, walking to the ground in the morning, having a couple of pints in the evening or occasionally going to the pictures. Death made regular trips home to see his family, more than most young players, as he was very close to his family and missed his home in the countryside. It was the same for Morgan, who says, 'To have him living across the road, walking to and from the training ground and going back to our digs together made such a difference to me. Having someone to say "see you in the morning" to, rather than just going up to my digs and being on my own, missing my mum and dad and my two brothers and two sisters at home in Swansea.'

Ron Greenwood and John Lyall encouraged the young players to watch as much football as possible, and Lyall or one of the other coaches would get them tickets. Steve's attitude was that rather than just wander around West Ham, they would pick a match somewhere in London they could get to on the tube or on the buses, taking in the atmosphere and watching matches wherever they could, whether at Leyton Orient, Tottenham, Arsenal, Chelsea, Millwall or Fulham. There were plenty of decent clubs around and it was a good education, as well as providing them with something to do. Death, as the senior partner as far as knowledge of London was concerned, would plan the routes to all the grounds, knowing which tube lines to travel on, and where the best pubs were. They took great comfort in being part of something and not having to fill in too much time on their own.

Breakfast in their digs was followed with a ten-minute walk to the ground and a bus to Chadwell Heath to the training ground. The place was still buzzing from the World Cup, and it was an amazing experience for them to be there with some of the greats of the game to look up to. Amid their dreams, however, there was also an awareness of the challenge facing them if they were to make it to the West Ham first team. As Morgan self-effacingly admits now, 'I was never going to replace Bobby Moore at centre-half,' but under Greenwood, the aim was to expose young players to the first-team environment so they could understand the level they would need to aim at.

Dave Llewellyn signed for West Ham in 1966, the year Death turned professional. Morgan joined in 1967. Llewellyn remembers Steve as both a great player and a great friend. 'He was so brilliant, he was so good, but he was a little bugger,' says Llewellyn now. 'He had the George Best looks, and all the women wanted him, but he just wasn't interested. As long as he had a cigarette and a beer, he was happy.

'He had every attribute you would look for. He was the best young goalkeeper I have ever seen. I played in the youth team with him, we went on tour and we won things. He was that good a player, he could do things you just wouldn't believe, saving shots he had no right to get to because he was so good at being in the right place to make the save. If there were people in front of him he could get them out of the way and get to the ball. Despite his size he would get to the crosses and high balls. He was such a good professional – although sometimes he didn't seem it! – and such a good goalkeeper. He would have made the England team without a doubt, he was that good. If you speak to any first-teamers at West Ham who saw him play, they would all say the same thing. I can't say any bad words about him.'

The three youngsters built a strong bond that saw them through their initial homesickness and carried them through their apprenticeships. Their shared dreams, similar backgrounds and tastes made them ideal companions as students at their football university, spending three seasons living, learning, talking, walking and drinking together. Their common bond initially kept them in London, and they became comrades in perhaps the most intense period of their lives.

'The club that won the World Cup'

Steve arrived at West Ham in 1965 and signed professional in 1966. It was an incredible club to join at the time, with the team on the crest of a wave, with legends everywhere he looked. West Ham had won the FA Cup in 1964, defeating Preston North End 3-2 at Wembley. They followed that up in 1965 by winning the European Cup Winners' Cup in another Wembley final, 2-0 against 1860 Munich. The third Wembley triumph in three years was the greatest of them all, England beating West Germany 4-2 with a hat-trick from Geoff Hurst, a goal from Martin Peters and brilliantly captained by Bobby Moore. All West Ham players, so the proud claim was that the Hammers were 'the club that won the World Cup'.

Upton Park was also the perfect place for a young footballer to learn his trade. With an established tradition of developing young players, including their three World Cup heroes, West Ham also claimed to be 'the Academy of Football'. Established in the 1950s under the then manager Ted Fenton, with his head coach Wally St Pier, the academy set about identifying the best young players in the area and giving them the best football education they could design. This included bonding the players off the pitch as well as on it, talking football for hours and immersing them in thinking about the game and ways they could improve as players.

Among the players scouted and developed by the academy of football were Bobby Moore, Geoff Hurst, Ken Brown, Malcolm Musgrove, Ronnie Boyce and Martin Peters. These were supplemented by a scouting system that spread its net further to bring in the likes of Noel Cantwell from Ireland, John Dick from Scotland, John Bond from Essex and Malcolm Allison from Kent. Allison took this on a step further while still a player and took the philosophy into his own high-profile management career.

By the time Steve Death joined, the academy was in the hands of one of the great managerial pioneers, Ron Greenwood, the man who had overseen the Wembley triumphs of 1964 and 1965 and provided Alf Ramsey with those three key players in 1966. Greenwood was a visionary coach, with a strong belief in the 'beautiful game'.

A capable centre-half who was on the fringes of the England team, Greenwood was in the stands for the landmark 6-3 Wembley defeat by the 'magical Magyars' of Hungary, Ferenc Puskás and all. The match has passed into legend as the day English football was jolted out of its complacency, the nation that invented the game being comprehensively thrashed by a foreign team playing football that seemed to come from another world.

Greenwood knew that football in England had to change. Players in training should do more than running laps around the pitch and doing exercises; they had to learn to love the ball. He took this philosophy to his first club management position as the first full-time professional manager of West Ham, and he started with the youngsters. Greenwood believed the future of the club came from the youth team. Everyone in that great West Ham team of the 1960s was home-grown.

Harry Redknapp describes Greenwood as being ahead of his time as a coach. He remembers the manager travelling with the youth team to an FA Youth Cup tie, leaving the first team to fend for itself in its First Division match on the same afternoon. He saw the 'kids' as that important. He knew every youth team member by name and was a constant presence at training, watching along with the coaches and discussing the progress of each player. Every Saturday that the senior team were playing at home, Greenwood would be present at Chadwell Heath to watch the youth team, staying as late as he physically could before he had to get to Upton Park to prepare the senior team. In that youth team, as it cut its competitive teeth in local cup competitions and gained experience on carefully curated foreign tours, Greenwood, John Lyall and the coaches scrutinised their young players, worked on their skills and analysed their characters, and developed a host of future first-teamers such as Billy Bonds, Pat Holland and Trevor Brooking.

Greenwood became aware of Steve Death when he watched his performance for England Schoolboys, and later said, 'I was instrumental in encouraging and signing him for West Ham United after his international exploits with England Schoolboys. After the first international game of the season, he kept out a young man called Peter Shilton and from then on he played in all the games for England and Peter was substitute. Stephen was one of the most athletic and agile goalkeepers that one would wish to see. He had a safe pair of hands and at the time of joining us he was quite small but one anticipated, naturally enough, that he would grow.'

The weekly training routine, typical of apprenticeships at the time, involved menial work alongside football and fitness drills. Apprentices were expected to help kit man Albert Walker as he placed the first team's kit in the dressing room before matches and sweep out the changing rooms and terraces afterwards. Other tasks such as painting the stands were not unusual; neither, of course, was being asked to clean the boots of the senior players. An apprentice's wage was £8 per week, plus £4 for lodgings and four-shilling vouchers for a local cafe.

On a typical day the apprentices would meet at Upton Park and be driven in the club's transit van to the Chadwell Heath training ground by youth team coach John Lyall. Before training they would put out the first team's training kit, and after training collect the soiled kit and take it back to be cleaned. This was common practice and was thought to be character-building as well as practical and thrifty for the club. The afternoons were free time for the young men to spend as they saw fit, and after lunch at Cassettari's Café to use their meal vouchers, typical activities included gym work for the more dedicated, games of head tennis back at Upton Park, and a trip to the cinema.

Evenings often involved a visit to a local hostelry, with the Two Puddings and the Black Lion in Plaistow favourite destinations for West Ham players. During one East End 'lock-in' at the Black Lion with Death, Morgan and Llewellyn in attendance, a car drew up outside at 2am and Bobby Moore's mum walked in to take him home.

Training often included practice matches between, for example, the youth and 'A' teams, or the reserves versus the first team. During training Greenwood would randomly call two or three youth players over to join the first team in a five-a-side or similar. This way, they would get to play with and against these great players on equal terms. He wanted the young players to understand what it was like in that environment and what was needed to play at that level. So Death would find himself keeping goal against the stars of the first team, in games that were every bit as competitive as a 'proper' match. Morgan remembers marking Geoff Hurst, and there would be 'elbows everywhere and arms in your face', posing the kind of challenge you wouldn't get from players at the same level as you. Harry Redknapp recalls one such game on a Thursday before a big match on the Saturday, in which Morgan 'nutted Geoff Hurst in the back of the head' after which Greenwood strategically withdrew the young centre-half from the game as he was 'dangerous'.

Never one for toeing the line or responding well to authority of any kind, the young goalkeeper was not afraid of challenging authority in his own calm and understated style. Apprentices would often be asked to perform various menial duties such as running the line in practice matches or putting out equipment, and as a young player Death accepted his place in the hierarchy and was happy to conform. What he would not do, it seems, was readily comply with rules and instructions he didn't see the point of. Llewellyn remembers a junior game when Greenwood asked him to take the drinks and other equipment, so he walked around with it and lit up a cigarette. The manager sent someone to tell him to put the cigarette out. Death's response was, 'Tell Ron to come and tell me himself.' 'That was Deathy,' says Llewellyn. 'He was such a nice fella but funny.'

While he took his job seriously enough, Death was never one for doing extra training and never showed any great interest or enthusiasm for working on technicalities. His was a natural talent and he more than made up for his lack of inches with his innate abilities. He had a great 'spring', enabling him to leap higher than opposing forwards and dispossess much taller strikers. He was also quick with great speed along the ground and could outrun anyone across the 18-yard box, closing forwards down before they had a chance to exploit his assumed weakness. While he was quiet off the pitch, and often described as a bit of a loner, on it he was a good talker, communicating well with his defence and, as Morgan said, 'Deathy would soon let you know' if he felt you needed his guidance.

Although the academy was in many ways ahead of its time, all training was led by the same core group of coaches, and they looked after all the players regardless of position. There was no such thing as specialist goalkeeping coaches so although former first-team keeper Ernie Gregory was on hand for the young Steve, he was also reserve-team coach, so the goalkeepers would normally spend some time on their own doing a spot of shooting practice.

When Death was picked to play for the West Ham youth side, opponents would often ask his team-mates, 'Are you sure he's a goalkeeper?' When the whistle blew, however, and he made a string of fine saves and caught their attempted lobs and crosses, they soon stopped asking.

Death's first appearance in a West Ham shirt was on 21 August 1965 as part of a youth XI which annihilated Charlton Athletic 9-1 in a South East Counties League match at Chadwell Heath. He played a total of 35 times for the youth side in his first season including a further 18 South East Counties League appearances and in a range of other competitions including the Metropolitan League, the FA Youth Cup where West Ham lost 1-0 to QPR in the quarter-final, and the Southern Junior Floodlight Cup, in which the Hammers reached the two-legged final where they ultimately lost to Arsenal.

Foreign tours and competitions were an important part of their football education, and the youth team took part in a competition in Switzerland, involving matches in Lucerne and Geneva in 1969, shortly before the end of Death's time at West Ham. They won the competition, with Death in goal and Morgan the captain. The team included Trevor Brooking and Frank Lampard, who then went on to join the under-21 side in a competition in Italy. Stuart Morgan remembers John Lyall coming up to him on the plane and handing him the trophy – an inscribed plate that he still has in his private collection. 'The trophy should have ended up in the West Ham boardroom, but Lyall gave it to me and said, "You've been magnificent in the tournament, you should have it." I don't think they'll miss it in the boardroom after all these years.'

Morgan sent me team photos of some of those sides, pointing out that Death was always pictured in the back row, in the traditional place for a goalkeeper, and that 'there would always be a big dip between the two centre-halves with Stevie in the middle'. Morgan says that from the outset Death was always a chain smoker. 'I kept saying to him, if you give them up maybe you'll grow a bit more!'

These were all great experiences for the young goalkeeper and everyone around the club started taking notice. In the following season he stepped up to the Football Combination (the old league for reserve teams), making his debut in a 0-0 draw with Ipswich Town at Portman Road on 11 March 1967. The West Ham website Forever Blowing Bubbles provides the underwhelming comment that this was a game in which 'excitement rarely occurred' as defences completely dominated and adds, 'It was Stephen Death's first Combination appearance and he did everything required of him.'

This was the season immediately following the World Cup win, and Upton Park was filled with optimism and pride. Death again played in the final of the Southern Floodlight Cup, appearing in a 2-1 first-leg win over Ipswich and sitting out a second-leg defeat in which his place was taken by Peter Grotier. In those gentlemanly times, the 3-3 aggregate scoreline meant both teams shared the trophy. In the following season, Death won his first professional trophy outright as his youth team beat Chelmsford City 6-4 on aggregate to win the same competition. By 1968/69 he was a regular in the reserves and made a total of 44 appearances across all competitions, including of course his First Division debut against Manchester City.

At this point, Death's quixotic side showed up again. He was informed by Ron Greenwood that England would like him to attend for trials with the under-19s. He simply said, 'No, I don't want to do that, Ron.' Dave Llewellyn tried to convince him, 'I told him he was mad, but he just didn't want to do it. He just said, "No, I don't want to do that, I don't want to go." I think he just loved playing the game but didn't want to go too far out of it. If he was bigger, Shilton would have had a fight on his hands to get a game, he was that good.'

Why Death took that stance no one can be really sure, but it fits with his approach to his entire career. His daughter Alex, when looking back on his time at Reading and speculating on why her dad had never agitated for a move to a 'better' club, said, 'I think he was happy just playing for Reading. He took his job very seriously and wanted to do it as well as he could. In his mind there was no way any forward was going to get past him, but he just wasn't interested in all the other stuff around it.' Perhaps he also knew that his size would mean he would never be chosen at the highest level, as proved to be the case at West Ham in the end.

Although a first-team player at the time, and a few years older than Death, Harry Redknapp was very much aware of the young stopper who had joined the club as an England Schoolboy international. Redknapp recalls, 'He was a one-off, a very laid-back guy. He used to like a fag and wasn't what you would describe as a mad keen goalkeeper or a super-fit athlete, but he had this great natural ability. He was a great lad, quiet, a real character and a real talent.'

A great judge of a player, who of course went on to have a hugely successful management career, Redknapp confirmed what everyone who saw Steve Death believed: if he had been 6ft 1in he would have played for England.

Playing with Death

Bobby Williams (1969-72)

A skilful inside-left, Bobby Williams played for his hometown club Bristol City from 1958-65, scoring an impressive 76 goals in 187 appearances. He is still remembered there with great fondness and is called upon to conduct stadium tours as a club legend. After spells at Rotherham United under Jack Mansell and then at Bristol Rovers, Mansell took him to Reading on a free transfer, where he scored 20 goals in 60 appearances and became club captain. After a spell as one of the first English footballers to play in Europe at AS Oostende in Belgium and a few games at Weymouth, Williams' career was ended by a car crash that almost killed him. He has been associated with Reading for over 50 years, as youth team manager and as a scout. Among his scouting successes was Jimmy Quinn (41 goals in his first season), after Stuart Morgan alerted him to his availability on a free from Bournemouth.

Brilliant goalkeeper. Small but when he jumped he was ten foot tall. He was magnificent in the air, and on the ground people used to shoot and he could judge and let it go past the post. Many a time I've said to him, 'Deathy, that was a bit close wasn't it?' He said, 'Didn't go in did it?' I said, 'No but it was close.' He said, 'Look, you go up there and score the goals and I'll keep them out this end.' That was Deathy.

He was fearless, he used to go down at people's feet. When we trained he didn't like to go in goal, he used to play out on the field when we played five-a-sides, and he used to kick lumps out of people. He used to love playing on the pitch. He would love it now when keepers can come out and pass the ball, I can see him now dribbling out of defence.

I played with a lot of goalkeepers, five at Bristol Rovers and three at Rotherham, and he was one of the best I ever played with.

He was quiet, one of the boys. He took all the banter. He just smiled and looked at you. He used to get nervous before a game. Jack would come up and ask, 'Deathy, you all right?' 'I'm all right, Jack,' he said. Barrie Wagstaff was another one who got nervous in those early days. Jack would say to them both, 'Go and have a fag,' so they'd go in the toilet have a couple of puffs of a cigarette and calm down. They were both nervous as kittens before a game. Stuart Morgan who came with him was a great lad. He loved Deathy. Stuart was hard as nails. He would kick anybody.

Deathy loved his greyhounds. He used to have a flat in Tilehurst Road at the ground and when I went to see him I had to step over two or three greyhounds to get in the front door. He loved his dogs; he loved his family.

He was a great keeper, a great lad. He used to go up and catch the ball with one hand. I still think of him now and I miss the old boy.

Les Chappell (1969-74)

Another inspired free transfer signing by Jack Mansell from Rotherham, striker Chappell played 201 times for Reading, scoring 78 goals, including 24 in his first season in 1969/70. He scored the fastest ever hat-trick for the club in nine minutes against Barnsley and still has the joint-highest number of hat-tricks for Reading, including four in a season in 1973/74. Chappell left in 1974, and following a spell at Doncaster Rovers he played in the first two promotion seasons as Swansea City went from the Fourth Division to the old First Division under John Toshack in the late 1970s. He stayed on as youth coach and was caretaker manager when Toshack left the club in 1984.

I used to give Stevie a lift from Elm Park, and later, Robin Friday. We would often train at Sonning Common, at the Adwest sports ground, and they both lived in club flats at Elm Park. I would be there waiting and waiting, and we were always late for training. They would keep me waiting half an hour. The manager would ask me, 'Where have you been, we've been here for ages?'

They were so different, those two. I remember Robin scoring against Rochdale and picking a policeman up and giving him a kiss. Whereas Stevie was very quiet, right from the moment he joined.

Jack Mansell signed him, and that first season was great fun to play in with an attacking team and with Jack's philosophy games were always exciting. I scored four hat-tricks.

He was a superb goalkeeper was Stevie, and a smashing lad. I remember how brave he was and how he would always go in where it hurt. It was a tough league in those days, and he made some terrific saves under pressure. He was a good professional and a good team man, and with all his ability he was not big-headed at all.

2

The Legend Begins – in the Third Division

Player of the year, while still on loan at Reading

IN STEVE Death's own words, 'After five years and only one first-team game, I wanted to get away and I was only too pleased to join Reading.' It was time to go. Death had played 159 times for West Ham's youth and reserve teams, toured with them, won trophies and trained and played with some of the game's greats. At 20, he was clearly not going to grow, so everyone around him would have to adjust their expectations.

Ron Greenwood, one of the most respected and innovative coaches of the 1960s and 70s, knew a good player when he saw one. He also recognised a good coach and had contacts throughout the game. One such contact was his great friend and coaching soulmate, Jack Mansell. Like Greenwood, Mansell had also been inspired by the legendary Hungarian team, having watched from the bench as they followed up their

6-3 win at Wembley by thrashing England 7-1 in Hungary. In November 1969, Mansell was managing Third Division Reading. He and Greenwood had taken FA coaching courses together and shared the same beliefs in how the game should be played. Mansell's Rotherham side had played attacking football and on joining Reading he had taken two vital players with him, striker Les Chappell and midfielder Bobby Williams, both on free transfers, who became their new club's leading scorer and team captain respectively.

Greenwood knew it was time to let Death go, and he knew that Mansell's Reading could be a perfect destination. It was a natural solution for both men, and both clubs, for Greenwood to send him out on loan to a manager he liked and respected. This is how Death and Stuart Morgan, two great friends who had shared three years at West Ham, where they had grown up together, arrived in Berkshire on the same day. Morgan – a former Welsh amateur boxing champion – was a tough-tackling centre-half, dominant in the air and on the ground, but was up against Bobby Moore in the queue for a first-team place, so moving on made perfect sense for him too. In the Third Division, both men could play regularly and make a difference.

Death and Morgan were signed in what the *Reading Chronicle* described as 'a dawn dash to London to sign two of West Ham's brightest young prospects'. Both were 19 years old, and fitted the bill for Mansell, who had already let

THE LEGEND BEGINS – IN THE THIRD DIVISION

11 players leave and signed six as he strove to transform an underachieving Reading team. New goalkeeper John Pratt had broken a leg in training – a personal tragedy for a 26-year-old former schoolteacher who had only just turned professional – and left Mansell lamenting, 'Now I must find a goalkeeper within the next few days.' The local press had already noted the glaring need for a 'powerhouse centre-half with a "thou shall not pass" mentality' and in Morgan the Reading manager found a player with 'an unflinching determination to win every ball' – a characteristic that had just led, in a reserve-team game, to him being the first West Ham player to be sent off since the Second World War. Mansell was undeterred and was delighted at signing two more important pieces in his jigsaw, building a strong defence as a launchpad for his attacking style.

The Reading that Steve joined could fairly be described as a natural Third Division club. Founded in 1871 and joining the Football League in 1920, Reading had never been big achievers. The closest they had come to glory was winning the Third Division South in 1925/26 and a 3-0 FA Cup semi-final defeat to eventual winners Cardiff City in 1927. The board of directors under chairman Frank Waller, a local businessman, kept a tight rein on the club's finances and it was difficult to discern any great ambition to be any more than they were.

Steve joined initially on a three-month loan, and after a topsy-turvy start to his Reading career he quickly became a firm favourite with both his new team-mates and his new supporters. If they could keep him permanently, they absolutely would. It turned out that they could, and they did, and he stayed with Reading for 13 years, making the most appearances of any goalkeeper in their history.

The two friends came straight into the side just two days after signing, making their debuts in a 1-0 win against Brighton & Hove Albion in a home game at Reading's Elm Park in front of 7,565 people. Death won rave reviews with the *Reading Evening Post* describing him as 'an insignificantly built bundle of daredevil agility. His positional play is decisive. One first-half save, low to his left from Kit Napier, was brilliant.' The *Reading Chronicle* agreed, writing, 'He has obvious class, positional sense and anticipation. His movements are decisive and he is abundantly confident.'

The pair had started with a clean sheet and a victory in Mansell's new-look defence, but the next two matches could not have been more challenging, or more different, starting with Southport away, where reality hit the new arrivals with a bang as Reading were hammered 6-2 before a crowd just over 2,000. Steve said, 'I had not met the Reading players before my first game and did not really know their names by the time we played Southport. I felt really sick after that game.'

Bobby Williams remembers the team sitting in the dressing room after the game in complete silence, heads down and feeling embarrassed and confused at the scale of their

THE LEGEND BEGINS - IN THE THIRD DIVISION

defeat. Mansell, however, simply walked into the room and said, 'Right, let's just forget about that one, shall we? Let's go and get some beer and fish and chips.' That was all he said on the matter – no tactical analysis, no inquest, just forget it and move on. It was a great example of his man-management skills and two days later, they turned it around by thumping Tranmere 5-1 for their biggest win of the season so far.

The Tranmere game was memorable for many reasons. It was a turning point in Reading's season as they then went on a 15-game unbeaten run that had them racing up the Third Division table, the result giving instant reassurance for Steve Death after letting in six against Southport in just his second match for his new club.

It was also the final match of Tommy Jenkins' short Reading career. Jenkins was another player who came to the club via Ron Greenwood, who had looked at him for two months on trial and couldn't make up his mind, so Mansell snapped him up for just £500 from non-league Margate, with a further £1,000 payable after ten first-team appearances. Jenkins was a mercurial talent, an excellent dribbler who his own team-mates found impossible to predict, and who was already attracting interest from First Division clubs. One of these, Southampton, watched him score a hat-trick against Tranmere and manager Ted Bates tabled a bid of £60,000 that Reading's board found impossible to turn down and he was gone after playing just 21 matches.

It was a nightmare evening for Stuart Morgan, who had joined with Death for £10,000, having impressed Mansell in a 14-game loan spell with Torquay at the end of the previous season. Like Death, he was playing in his third game for Reading, lining up in front of him at centre-half in a defence that was still bedding in. Morgan was injured late in the first half. It was a serious injury to his ankle, but he was simply strapped up at half-time and asked to stand on the right wing for the second half and 'be a nuisance'.

Having spent the rest of the game hobbling around on the wing, still undiagnosed and untreated, Morgan was dropped off by the team coach at a north London tube station in the early hours of the following morning. As they both still lived in their old digs at West Ham, Death was dropped there with him. It soon became clear to both men that Morgan wasn't going anywhere with his ankle in such a state.

'Stevie was magnificent,' says Morgan now, 'and showed me how strong he was that night when he carried me on his back across to Upton Park and our digs.' The 5ft 7.5in goalkeeper carried the 6ft 2in, 13 stone centre-half through the dark London streets, making sure he got him back home safely. Morgan continues, 'Steve did the same thing, after a little sleep, carrying me to Upton Park the next morning, where we met the furious physio Rob Jenkins. He was straight on the phone to Elm Park and put Reading's physio Jimmy Wallbanks to the sword about the treatment that had been dished out to me.' Jenkins then arranged for a taxi ride to hospital to learn the inevitable – Reading's new signing had broken his ankle in just his third game, played on for the entire second half, and been dropped off in the middle of the night, to be carried home on the slight shoulders of his team-mate and friend.

While Morgan was unable to start another match until being chosen as the right-back for a 5-0 away defeat at league leaders Luton at the end of March, Mansell wasted no time in replacing the departed Tommy Jenkins, going straight to Arsenal to spend £12,000 of the Jenkins fee on their reserve-team winger Gordon Cumming, and £10,000 on Hull left-back Dennis Butler, both of whom slotted into the team in early December. In his first full season in charge, Mansell generated almost £100,000 in transfer fees and spent £50,000. Both were far in excess of any season before and a newspaper review of 1969 estimated that the transfer income was more than the club had earned in its entire history up to that point. Reading had never seen anything like it.

Cumming was a catalyst for Reading's strong finish to the season and became a fixture in the team. Bobby Williams, an experienced and skilful midfielder and a great leader, highlights another link between Reading and Ron Greenwood: this time a tactical one. Mansell was another early exponent of a classic West Ham and England training ground move – the near-post cross. Most teams, he says, favoured the traditional high ball to the big centre-forward, but Reading perfected the low, hard near-post cross. Cumming excelled at this skill, and the routine practised in training led to a glut of goals as defenders were caught napping, beaten to the ball by the quick forward line. In the World Cup Final and in the First Division, Martin Peters crossed for Geoff Hurst to score. For Reading, Gordon Cumming fired in cross after cross for Les Chappell to score. Williams says, 'If it didn't get to Les, Dick Habbin followed up, and if Dick couldn't reach it, I was there to score.' Chappell scored 24 goals that season, Habbin nine and Williams 16.

Williams now calls Mansell 'the best manager Reading ever had' and says, 'We played some great football that season. His attitude was, "If they score one we'll score two; if they score two we'll get three." That was his philosophy. He liked to attack. Jack had us playing triangles. He used to say to me as a midfielder to just go and get the ball and pass it. "You know what to do, just go out and do it." We couldn't wait to get out there.'

Reading's leading scorer under Mansell was Les Chappell, who was with him and Williams at Rotherham. Chappell shares his team-mate's opinion of their old manager. 'Jack was funny,' he says. 'One of my first games for Reading under Jack, Ray Henderson was the coach. We won 2-0 and Ray said to Jack, "Look at Les, he only had two touches and scored two goals!" and Jack said, "What do you think I bought him for?" He liked us to play one-touch, two-touch and his instruction

THE LEGEND BEGINS – IN THE THIRD DIVISION

to me was when the final ball comes into the box, that's your job, you get on the end of it, and that's what I did.'

Chronicle reporter Roger Ware spent a lot of time around the management and staff at Reading and knew Mansell well. 'Jack was very opinionated,' says Ware. 'When a board member he had no respect for came into his office after a game once and said, in what Jack considered to be a condescending way, "How are you? How are the team?" Mansell said, "You don't give a damn how I am or anyone else here, and when you come in here next time, will you please have the goodness to knock first?" He wouldn't talk football with anyone who didn't understand the game, and couldn't tolerate the board, which was eventually to be his downfall.'

In March of that season Reading were at home against Luton. Reading were fourth and on a 15-game unbeaten run and league leaders Luton featured a young centre-forward in Malcolm Macdonald who was taking the division by storm. It was a foggy evening and there was heavy traffic leading to the compact Elm Park ground, which was in a densely populated residential area in Tilehurst Road, hemmed in by terraced houses and roads on every side. Death had spent the afternoon with Dave Llewellyn, his old friend from West Ham, and driving to the match in Llewellyn's car, they found themselves stuck among the almost 19,000 fans flocking to the ground in low visibility as part of the biggest home attendance of the season.

While Llewellyn tried to get Reading's star goalkeeper to the ground on time, it became obvious that they weren't going to make it. Bobby Williams remembers the game well, 'It was quarter past seven and we heard that Deathy was stuck in traffic. Tony Wagstaff went to Jack Mansell and said, "What are we going to do?" Wagstaff was nervous about playing the league leaders with only ten men, but the manager was clear. Mansell replied, "We'll play without him until he comes. We can hold these until Deathy gets here." Mansell asked for a volunteer to go in goal and our full-back Dennis Butler volunteered. We played for ten minutes until Deathy arrived. That's how much we thought of him, that we were prepared to wait for him rather than risk playing the whole game without him.'

Reading more than held their own against their promotion-seeking rivals, eventually losing to a last-minute goal scored after a powerful surge through their defence by Macdonald. Luton finished the season in second place, with the Royals ending up just seven points behind them in eighth.

The Reading public were treated to a run of high-scoring games that season with a clutch of 3-2 victories and other scores of 4-1, 6-3 and 6-2 (featuring a nine-minute hat-trick from leading scorer Les Chappell at home to Barnsley). At 3-2 up against Bury, Williams looked up at the big old clock above the stand at Elm Park and saw that they had only been playing for 20 minutes and said to himself, 'We'd better slow down!' Against Barrow, he remembers that Reading were 5-0 up and Barrow suddenly went 'bang, bang, bang' and it was 5-3. As they took the kick-off after Barrow's third goal, Reading striker Dick Habbin turned to Williams and said, 'We'd better score another one now,' and they went straight down the other end and scored a sixth. The season finished perfectly with an 8-0 revenge win over the Southport team who had made Reading's new goalkeeper feel sick just five months before.

It had been a great first season for Death, playing competitive games twice a week in a richly talented, attacking side playing devil-may-care football that kept him and his defence exceptionally busy. After missing only one league match since his arrival in November, he was voted player of the year by Reading supporters. This after only 28 matches. He was still on loan.

That 8-0 victory against Southport on the final day of the season was the perfect last act in a season of fluent, attacking and incisive football. It also set up a highlight in the career of every member of that team, and a special memory for every Reading fan of a certain vintage. The Watney Cup was a new competition for the highest-scoring team in each of the four divisions who had not won a title or promotion. With their huge win over Southport, Reading reached a mammoth 87 goals for the 1969/70 season, the highest not just in the Third Division but the entire Football League, and this qualified them for the inaugural Watney Cup, to be played in August as a curtain-raiser for the following season. Reading were drawn to play Manchester United, just two years after they had become the first English team to win the European Cup.

At the end of the season Death went back to West Ham as his transfer had still not been finalised, so he was still officially their player when he returned to Reading for pre-season. Reading wanted him but finding the £20,000 fee was proving to be quite a task.

Reading too good for Third Division?

Reading 2 Manchester United 3
Reading: Death, Dixon, Butler, Bell, Morgan, Barrie Wagstaff, Cumming, Chappell, Habbin, Tony Wagstaff, Williams

Manchester United: Stepney, Edwards, Dunne, Crerand, Ure, Sadler, Morgan, Law, Charlton, Kidd, Best

Season 1970/71 started on a high for Steve Death and Reading, with Manchester United sending their strongest team to Elm Park on a blazing August day. The legendary trinity of George Best, Denis Law and Bobby Charlton were in town. In truth only Charlton played well, turning in a masterful performance to run United's midfield and score two trademark goals. As captain Bobby Williams says, 'I shook his hand before the game and that was the closest I got to him all afternoon!' Best had a quiet game and Law was feeling his way back from injury, but for the fans of a Third Division side to see so many great players and such an iconic team was unforgettable.

For all that it was dressed up as a competition it was in essence a pre-season friendly, but it felt to everyone involved like an important game and the crowd of 18,348 was testament to the drawing power of Reading's glamorous opponents. Stuart Morgan still has a copy of a photograph from the match, in which he appears behind Death and Best as they compete for the ball, with Law and Brian Kidd waiting to pounce. His copy is signed 'To Stuart, Best wishes, George Best'.

ITV gave it the full treatment with a 20-minute highlights package on *The Big Match* with commentary from Brian Moore and an expert panel including Pat Crerand (who was in the United team that day) and Malcolm Allison, chaired by Jimmy Hill. Hill even compared Reading to the Brazil team who had just won the 1970 Mexico World Cup and at the end of the programme he presented an analysis comparing the saves made by Death and the United keeper Alex Stepney, showing both the threat of the Reading attack and the skills of their goalkeeper. United won 3-2, with Paul Edwards adding to Charlton's double, while Reading's goals came from Dick Habbin and Gordon Cumming.

Death had by now been officially transfer-listed by West Ham, and the publicity generated by his performance in the United match proved to be the final push the Reading board needed to stump up his transfer fee and prevent another side from moving in on their on-loan goalkeeping sensation, so the money was found and his transfer went through in time for the new season.

Charlton had a weekly column in *Goal* magazine, and the headline the following week read 'READING TOO GOOD FOR THIRD DIVISION' above an article in which he waxed lyrical about the Royals, how skilful they were and how difficult they had made the afternoon for United. Charlton predicted that Reading would have a great season and would be challenging for promotion to the Second Division. Sadly, that was as good as it would get and Reading proved Charlton wrong in spectacular fashion, celebrating their centenary season by being relegated to the Fourth Division for the first time in their history.

It was a dismal season in which everything that could go wrong did go wrong. The cavalier football of the previous season was still there at times, but the team forgot how to score as well as defend, while Death missed almost half the campaign through injury, playing in only 27 matches out of 46. However, it would be hard to argue that the lack of game time for the goalkeeper was a deciding factor in the season, as in one six-match spell in March and April the team had no wins, one draw and five defeats, scoring once and conceding 15. This was part of a collapse in form in the second half of the season that saw them nosedive into the relegation zone.

In all, Reading managed to score just 40 times, conceding 85 to finish the season with a mammoth goal difference of minus 45. Relegation came about in the most wretched possible way, in a final game away to Aston Villa, delayed because of Villa's success in reaching the League Cup Final. A headed own goal by centre-forward and leading scorer Terry Bell with seconds remaining denied them the single point they needed to stay up. Bell claimed he had been pushed in the back as he attempted to clear a corner. Bobby Williams, sitting in the stands, turned to the person next to him and said, 'Well, that's just got me a free transfer.' He was right, and Reading were now a Fourth Division team.

Playing with Death

Gordon Cumming (1969-78)

Signed for £12,000 from Arsenal, Cumming appeared over 300 times for Reading - the only club he played for at senior level, scoring 61 goals. Bought to replace the mercurial Tommy Jenkins, Cumming proved to be an important player for Reading, and was a key member of the team that won the club's first promotion for 50 years, in 1976. The former winger and later midfielder still lives in the town and goes to Reading matches home and away with his grandson.

We used to train at the Adwest sports ground in Sonning. Charlie Hurley was the manager and Maurice Evans was there as his assistant. We used to run from there past the cricket ground in Sonning Common and on to Henley Road. As we ran up the hill past Shiplake College there was a pub, and Maurice would be there to tick us all off on his list as we ran past. Then there was no one else between the cricket ground and the pub.

Me and my mate Dick Habbin used to really go for it and try to get as fit as we could. We were running as hard as we could when all of a sudden this tractor goes past and sitting in the back was John Murray, Stevie Death and Robin Friday, smiling and waving at us. They got dropped off in just the right place and waited for a decent amount of time until they could feasibly finish the run without appearing to win, which would have been suspicious.

John Murray was sacked in the middle of the season by Bury for indiscipline, and a football contact of Charlie's recommended him. Charlie took him on, thinking he could change him, but you will never change a player like that.

Training-wise, well, it was non-existent really. But at that time there wasn't the professionalism there is now, it was down to you if you wanted to get fit or not. Mostly we travelled to away games and back on the same day to save money, usually in an old Smith's coach, but I remember a match at Hartlepool away when we travelled up on a Friday. Someone phoned Charlie and told him how good we were. He told them that we only drank halves, which was true, we did only drink halves – but we didn't let on how many!

We were walking back from a pub the night before another away game, this time at Torquay, and there was a hotel with one of those high awnings, hanging from scaffolding above the door. Deathy ran up to it, took a flying leap and headed it. But there was concrete behind it, and he had headed it really hard. He fell on the floor in agony and the rest of us were falling about laughing, with poor old Deathy almost dying on the floor – our goalkeeper for the next day.

It takes all different characters to make a team. I was dedicated, a lot of people were, but a lot of people weren't. Tommy Youlden for example didn't have an ounce of fat on his body. We would all be at the front of the coach and Deathy would be at the back with a little clique including Dunphy, Friday and Murray. There were no big names in our team then, we were mostly free transfers like Les Chappell and Bobby Williams, and there was only money for Deathy, me and people like Dennis Butler because of selling Tommy Jenkins for such a big fee.

3

Life in the Basement

Life as a Fourth Division footballer in the 1970s, and how Reading gained their first promotion in 50 years

THAT FIRST season in the Fourth Division, although ultimately a poor campaign, did have one major highlight. This was an FA Cup run in which Reading, with Steve Death in goal, reached the fourth round by beating non-league side Bridgewater Town in the first round, local rivals Aldershot in the second, and more non-league opposition in Blyth Spartans in round three. Following a 2-2 draw away at Blyth both sides knew that the prize for the winners was a home tie against the double-winning Arsenal side in round four. Reading had been 2-0 up and cruising when Blyth scored two goals in the last ten minutes, played in near darkness as they had no working floodlights. The replay at Reading was played in the afternoon after a request from their amateur opponents, who were worried that their part-time players would have to cope with a long journey home overnight and miss out on the next day's work if the game was played in the evening. Reading won the replay 6-1 and for the second time in less than two years found themselves playing one of the best teams in the land.

Reading 1 Arsenal 2

Reading: Death, Butler, Dixon, Morgan, Wooler, B. Wagstaff, Harley, Harman, Cumming, Habbin, Chappell

Arsenal: Wilson, Nelson, Rice, McLintock, Simpson, Armstrong, Ball, Kelly, Kennedy, George, Graham

The FA Cup was then universally seen as not just the oldest but the best cup competition in the world, and it would be decades before any manager would even think about not playing his best available team for a cup tie at any stage of the competition. Steve Death would be facing Arsenal, the winners of the First Division and the FA Cup the previous season, knowing they would be going all out to defend the trophy. The full-strength Gunners included Death's opposite number Bob Wilson and stars such as George Armstrong, Charlie George, Alan Ball and George Graham, and a capacity crowd of 25,756 came to see if little Reading could do the impossible.

What they saw was a barely believable afternoon of football in which Reading outplayed their illustrious visitors for large parts of the match and competed with them on equal terms throughout. Reading famously scored three times in the match. The only problem was that two of those were in the wrong net and they ended up losing 2-1.

A long-range shot from Pat Rice cannoned off the shoulder of midfielder Jon Harley to give Arsenal the lead, leaving Death wrong-footed and with no chance of doing anything other than watching the ball sail into the far corner. Reading's equaliser was a brilliant long-range effort from midfielder Barry Wagstaff that dipped under Wilson's crossbar, but fate had one more twist in the game. Death's old mate Stuart Morgan, back in the team after yet another injury, flung himself at a near-post corner and sent a bullet header past his own goalkeeper to give Arsenal their win.

Morgan's recollection of the Arsenal game is dominated by the own goal, which he recalled with total clarity over 50 years later, 'We played our hearts out that day. I followed the ball and ran to the near post. I was determined to be first there and keep it out, but I just forgot where it was in relation to the 18-yard box. It was a great header, and if it wasn't for the net it would still be travelling now.'

Years later he was shopping in the arcade in Bournemouth with his wife when he spotted Bob Wilson with his wife. Morgan went over to him and said, 'You won't remember me, I'm Stuart Morgan, I played against you in the FA Cup.' 'Ah yes,' said Wilson. 'The own goal!'

By the time Arsenal came to town, Jack Mansell had been replaced as manager by Charlie Hurley. Mansell had been sacked in October of that first season in the Fourth Division, after a run of four goalless games. At their best, his teams had entertained, producing fanciful scorelines with goals at both ends, but after a low-scoring season in the Third Division and a grim start to the new campaign, the board had run out of patience. After a long recruitment process, with no fewer than 53 applicants to sift through, chairman Frank Waller chose Hurley above the Manchester United European Cup winner Bill Foulkes. According to Hurley, he sealed the job straight after his third interview, when Waller and he bumped into each other in the gents' toilet at Elm Park. Waller told Hurley that it was hard to choose between him and Foulkes, and Hurley quipped that if Reading wanted to make the wrong decision, they should choose Foulkes. Waller laughed and the job offer was made in a short phone call that same weekend.

Hurley set about producing a more disciplined side with a new and much-needed emphasis on building play from a solid defence. However, having arrived with the team in 14th place, he was unable to make any real impact and they finished the season 16th, just one position and two points above local rivals Aldershot, scoring 56 times and conceding 78.

Towards the end of the season, Death was hit by personal tragedy. On 8 April 1972, the day after a 4-1 away defeat to Southend United, football paled into insignificance when his beloved mum died suddenly at the very young age of 42.

Devastated by her death, and the knowledge that she would never know his unborn child, he went back to Suffolk to see her buried. It was a bitter blow for the devoted son who had travelled back home as often as he could as a young player at West Ham, and who continued to be close to her as he started his own family and progressed in his chosen career.

Stuart Morgan left the club at the end of the season, summing up the transitory life of the professional footballer in the days when his fate was usually decided by their employers with little or no input from them: 'We drifted away, never really said "cheerio" to each other. That's the sad part. You're there one day and the next you're off to another club. I had about five clubs, but he [Death] was a one-club man. We lost touch perhaps sooner than we should have done once I left Reading. Charlie Hurley came in and it all changed.'

Reading remained a Fourth Division side for the next four years. Success continued to elude them in the next three seasons as they finished seventh, eighth and seventh again, at times threatening to challenge for promotion but always falling short.

Hurley was a genuine hero to supporters of Sunderland, to whom he was simply known as the King. He was voted the club's player of the century for his 400 appearances as a dominant and skilful centre-half, and a 2008 biography was subtitled 'the greatest centre-half the world has ever seen' using the words of the supporters' song.

On the day of his appointment, Hurley told the local press, 'I am sure I can do some good here. I am a great believer in discipline, hard work and the need for players and managers to be professional.' Writing for the *Evening Post*, David Dibben suggested that Hurley's experience with less prosperous and successful clubs had given him the edge over Foulkes. If so, Hurley would need all of that experience in the months and years to come.

In the first 18 matches of the 1972/73 season, Reading conceded just 11 goals, and in the first year of Hurley's management they went from having the worst defence in the Fourth Division to the best in all four divisions of the Football League. The contrast with the free-wheeling, attack-minded Jack Mansell could not have been clearer.

From speaking to some of his Reading team now, it's clear that Hurley's legacy is perhaps viewed more ambiguously, due in large part to the challenges he faced as the only visible target for their frustration with a penny-pinching board of directors; however, no one could dispute his passion for the cause. One local journalist experienced this passion first hand when he approached him for comment on the referee after a particularly frustrating game away to Grimsby. Hurley delivered the following assessment, 'You want my opinion of the referee? I think he's a fucking great ponce who deserves a kick in the fucking balls.' When writing up his post-match interview, the journalist reported his comment a little more diplomatically as 'the Reading manager was unimpressed with the referee's performance'.

However, a highlight of 1972/73, Hurley's first full season in charge, was another FA Cup adventure. This one took Reading away to Sunderland in a third-round tie that brought Hurley back to Roker Park and the fans who still adored him. The scene that greeted the Reading players when they walked on the pitch before the game to assess what studs to wear, with thousands of fans chanting Hurley's name, made a huge impression on them. Hurley used his own reception in his team talk, telling his players that they had to give the game the biggest amount of fight they had ever given. 'You're representing me,' he said. 'If you don't fight you won't play for me any more.' Fight they did, coming agonisingly close to winning. If they had, Sunderland's historic FA Cup Final victory over Don Revie's great Leeds United team would never have happened, and Bob Stokoe's trilby would have been denied its 15 minutes of fame.

Roger Ware of the *Reading Chronicle* was at Roker Park commentating for hospital radio. He recalled, 'We agreed with Sunderland that I could do a commentary from the touchline, by the Reading dugout. I saw at first hand just how much love the Sunderland fans had for King Charlie, the massive ovation as he walked down the touchline and, despite local loyalties, wishing him well for the game. Even though he was obviously engrossed in the tactical needs of the game, Charlie still found time to offer those in hospital back in Reading his insights into the chances of getting a favourable result. In the end, "favourable" it was, a hard-earned 1-1 draw.'

If Sunderland v Reading was a watershed moment for Hurley, it was also a memorable one for Steve Death. David Dibben, writing in the *Evening Post*, said that 'in 15 years of watching Reading it was easily the best goalkeeping performance I have ever seen'.

Reading took the lead with a first-half goal that was another product of the Greenwood/Mansell and, indeed, Alf Ramsey near-post move, Les Chappell expertly guiding in a cross from Gordon Cumming. Fired up by the famous Roker Roar, the home side then threw everything they had at their Fourth Division opponents. Death was equal to it all, or at least he was until an uncharacteristic fumble allowed Dennis Tueart to pounce on the rebound and equalise in the 71st minute. Despite his great performance, Death could only dwell on the mistake that denied his team a major cup upset; a very human reaction but a harsh one after such a display of skill and commitment. Hurley himself said, 'Stephen Death the goalkeeper was magnificent. He was a great lad.'

Hurley's 'great lad' was in his pomp that year, an ever-present in all Reading's 48 matches and conceding only 38 times. He was helped by a miserly defence in which Tommy Youlden, a Hurley signing, joined the defence inherited from the former manager. Reading had gone from having the worst defence in the Fourth Division to having the best defensive record in the professional game.

At the end of the season, Death was awarded his second player of the year prize from the Elm Park faithful. He repeated the feat the following season, ending 1973/74 as an ever-present again, conceding just 37 times and being voted player of the year for a third time. His achievements were also recognised by his fellow professionals as he was chosen as the best goalkeeper in the division by the PFA, an award voted for by the players who had found him so hard to score against during the season.

In his programme notes following a hard-fought 1-0 win at home against Barnsley in March 1974, Charlie Hurley commented on a crucial save Death had made, without which 'we really would have had a fight on our hands'. He wrote, 'Our back four have said that they always let the opposition have one good shot at our goal just to keep Steve on his toes. I leave you to work out whether you believe this or not.'

In the supporters' club notes section of the programme in April that year they congratulated him on his 100th consecutive first-team appearance. In the previous 99 games Steve had let in a mere 87 goals and in 46 of those he kept a clean sheet – a remarkable feat even for the best goalie in the Fourth Division. By the end of that game his record read 100 consecutive appearances, with 87 goals conceded and 47 clean sheets.

Reading were a solid team, finishing in the top half of the table each season, close to the promotion places but never serious contenders. In the following season, 1974/75, Death and his defence again conceded fewer goals than they played games, but still finished five points off the final promotion place and 16 points behind champions Mansfield Town.

Death's first three years at Reading had brought him more brushes with legends, following his early football education in training and, once, playing with Hurst, Peters and Moore. A match against Manchester United, fielding essentially the team that won the European Cup, had quickly followed, and double winners Arsenal completed the set. Sandwiched between United and Arsenal, however, was relegation and Death was now a Fourth Division player. Relegated by an own goal in the last seconds of the season, knocked out of the FA Cup by two own goals in one game; life at Reading was certainly not dull.

Life as a Fourth Division footballer in the 1970s was full of contradictions. You could be a hero to thousands, hear your name chanted from the terraces, share in and create some of the best and most emotional experiences of their lives and yet be unknown to the wider world. Training sessions were held in various local parks and sports grounds, with people walking past and paying little or no attention, while long-distance running took the players along public roads and through villages. If you were considered an important player, you would be pressed for quotes about next Saturday's game and read speculation about the state of your groin or hamstring. You could also be stopped by young fans with autograph books or asked to visit supporters and their families in hospital. All of this while earning a weekly wage that in most cases was less than the earnings of a skilled or semi-skilled worker on a building site.

One of Death's team-mates, Gordon Cumming, a senior player and an automatic first-team choice since joining from Arsenal in 1969, found a practical and lucrative way to top up his earnings, making use of the time a footballer could have on his hands after finishing training for the day.

'We would be on £40 a week and the chippie or plumber up the road would be on 50 or 60,' says Cumming. 'We didn't do it for the money, it was for the love of the game. We enjoyed it. When I played and the Deaths, Murrays and all that went to the pub after training I went to a building site where I knew a guy who played for a local amateur team who was a painter. "What do you do in the afternoons?" he asked me one day. Nothing. "Can you paint?" The painter was lazy and said just turn up whenever you want and do some painting and I'll give you a pound an hour. He was never there; he didn't want to paint and I used to turn up for three or four hours in the afternoon and do his painting for him. Eventually, the builder in charge of the site noticed that I was doing all the work and he was paying somebody else who wasn't turning up, so he got rid of the guy and offered me a job whenever I had time. He employed me to do some labouring, help the chippie with the roof, help the brickies and do whatever I could. That kind of work became my job for years after I finished football.'

Another way for a few players to earn some extra cash was to write a column for the local paper. Cumming also exploited this way of subsidising his weekly wage, but while his work in the building trade was based on his practical skills, his writing was not based on any journalistic talent or ambitions whatsoever. Cumming told me, 'The club captain used to write a piece for the *Reading Chronicle* every week. David Dibben, who reported on all things Reading for rival paper the *Evening Post*, suggested I write a column for them. I couldn't write like that, so I used to make a few notes, for example on the offside rule, and Dibben would turn it into something that looked like a newspaper article. Dibben would check it with the club secretary to make sure I wasn't libelling anyone and then it would get published in the paper on a Friday.'

The most famous example of this was Eamon Dunphy, whose weekly column in the *Reading Evening Post* was genuinely and entertainingly written by the player himself. In Dunphy's case this led to a post-football career in writing and punditry as he went on to write best-selling biographies of the rock band U2 (*Unforgettable Fire*) and Sir Matt Busby (*A Strange Kind of Glory*). His chronicle of half a season in the

Second Division with Millwall, *Only a Game?*, had already been written before he signed for Reading.

Dunphy, a key member of the Reading team that finally won promotion to the Third Division, has argued in writing that for a player to play in the Fourth Division inevitably meant 'there was something wrong with him' – that there must be a flaw in the player that prevented him from making the grade at a higher level. Dunphy exempted himself from this assessment, of course, arguing that coming to Reading meant he was taking a step down that he didn't need to make. As a former Eire international and a regular for Second Division Millwall he had signed on to help Charlie Hurley, a former international team-mate, to deliver success in his first managerial position for a club with no history of achievement. He went on to claim that if it wasn't for him and for Gordon Cumming, Reading would not have achieved what they did.

The counter-argument has already been put forward by Stuart Morgan in his comments earlier in this book, that forging a career in the Football League was something to be proud of. Every player interviewed for this book has enjoyed looking back on their career with pride and nostalgia for a great period of their lives, with an instinctive understanding of the satisfaction of doing an important job well, creating memories, and being part of something greater than themselves. Only a very few people out of the thousands of talented hopefuls make it to the Football League at all, and often it is a simple twist of fate that separates the Fourth Division player from someone in the First Division, such as Gordon Cumming breaking his collarbone in a reserve match when on the verge of the Arsenal first team or Stuart Morgan being understudy to Bobby Moore.

After five years in the Fourth Division, and 50 years since the club had won any kind of honour at all, Charlie Hurley finally built the promotion-winning team of 1975/76. It was put together on the proverbial shoestring; a combination of experienced, hardened old pros, a couple of whom were drinking in the last chance saloon, and the odd youngster. It was full of character and of 'characters', both of which are essential to a successful team in any walk of life. You need the quiet ones, the mavericks, the selfless and the egotistical, the hard-bitten, cynical old pros and the eager young ones with everything to prove, the lasting friendships and the niggling rivalries: Reading 1975/76 had all of that and more. Ask anyone who lived through that time to name them and they will have little difficulty in coming up with the regular 11, and even some of the fringe players, but everyone starts with two names, usually in this order: Robin Friday and Steve Death.

How a small Fourth Division club came to have two such generational talents in the same team is a minor miracle. It is also another reason why lower-league football should be cherished, as the memories conjured by these two players are special to everyone involved who was lucky enough to share those few seasons that they were in the same team. Both were blessed with a rare natural talent, both were individuals on and off the pitch, and both were talked about with no hyperbole as players who were good enough to play for England. Both also had characteristics that prevented them from doing so. For Death it was of course his height. For Friday it was his character and behaviour.

Let's start, as everyone does, with Robin Friday. Charlie Hurley first became aware of him when Reading faced Hayes in December 1972, the non-league team forcing a replay after a 0-0 draw and eventually losing 1-0 to their Fourth Division opponents. Friday couldn't score in either match, but he did manage to leave his mark on Reading's goalkeeper in more ways than one. Firstly, he gave Death a kick on the thigh that left him too stiff to immediately take the free kick given for the foul; to add insult to injury, the referee interpreted his slowness as deliberate time-wasting and booked him.

Friday played in both games, and Hurley went to watch him several times over the next year. Hurley was impressed by his play but researched his background and was put off by his off-field lifestyle, as were so many others who scouted him as he made such an impact in the Isthmian League. He learned that Friday reportedly drank heavily, did drugs and womanised, and had a spell in borstal in his teens for theft. He was sent off seven times while at Hayes, but also scored 46 goals for them in 67 appearances. His ability was unquestioned, however, and Hurley eventually took the plunge and signed him in January 1974 for a fee of £750.

In the early days, Friday was signed as an amateur, but it quickly became clear what an impact he was having on his new club and he soon signed professional amid both formal and informal interest from other clubs, including an opposition player coming on as a substitute with a coded message from his manager that he would like to sign him. When signing professional terms, Friday was coerced by Hurley into wearing a suit jacket for the official photo call in front of the local press. Friday tried in vain to escape from this affront to his preferred dress code but managed to negotiate not to wear the tie also proffered to him by his manager. In keeping with life at Fourth Division Reading, Friday's weekly wage was less than he had previously earned from his work as an asphalter, but this was, finally, his route into professional football.

Friday was a complete one-off and quickly became a cult hero, initially at Reading, then in his short-lived spell at Cardiff City. His status as a poster boy for wayward talent and nonconformity continued long after his brief career, in the 1997 book of recollections of him, *The Greatest Footballer You Never Saw* by Paul McGuigan and Paolo Hewitt; on the cover of a Super Furry Animals CD; and in two novels by Paul Kane. His off-field antics raised eyebrows, and not just among the stuffy elements of football boardrooms. He was banned from local pubs such as the Boar's Head in the town centre multiple times, only to charm them into changing their minds when he had sobered up.

Hurley had to withdraw him from the five-a-side game in his first training session with the club as he went around kicking all the established players and the manager feared having no one left to play in the first team at the weekend. He went on to do things in his own way, keeping to his own unique sense of time, having liquid lunches, and doing the odd disappearing act, including being late for pre-season training after joining a drug-fuelled free-love commune in close-season without thinking to inform anyone at the club. As time wore on Hurley began to tire of covering up his star player's increasingly obvious drug-taking.

As a player though, Friday's team-mates loved him. Writing in his *Reading Evening Post* column, Dunphy wrote what was in effect a love letter to his team-mate, 'Robin Friday is unique. It is difficult to measure his influence on our side, for one has to take into account not only his talent as a player but the sheer power of his presence which invariably intimidates his opponents and is a source of inspiration to us lesser mortals who play with him.

'Robin is good enough to play at any level of the game. He would be just as potent a force in the First Division, a thought which prompts the question – what is he doing in the Fourth Division? The answer lies in the wild, extravagant nature of the man and the prejudices of many leading managers whose ideal player is a lion on the field and a lamb off it. Robin Friday, the player, would be welcome at any club. Robin Friday, the citizen, would cause many to cringe.'

John Turner recounts one occasion when the players were talking about their talisman, 'I remember Eamon Dunphy saying this, "You will read in the papers, Robin Friday found in the gutter with a knife in his back, dead. He won't reach 40." As a young kid I thought, why is he saying that? Amazing, how experience tells.'

As Dunphy predicted, Friday's lifestyle off the pitch was destined to cut short his career and ultimately did cost him his life but, for the two and a half years he was with the club, and this season in particular, the balance was still very much in favour of his actions on the pitch. And what actions they were.

As defender Tommy Youlden says now, 'He didn't live like a footballer, he lived like a pop star. But he was an unbelievable player to have in your team, the things he could do with the ball. If you got the ball to him, not only could he do great things and score goals, he had so much skill he could take the pressure off the whole team.'

Full-back Gary Peters describes Friday as 'such a brilliant player and such a nutcase. Every other club knew so much about him and had to find a way of stopping him playing. He used to drop deep and they didn't know how to pick him up. He was so good we just learned to play around him, and the more experienced players filled in and did the other bits so

Robin could get on with taking the world on. If he could have been someone who could live in a normal way he could have gone right to the top.'

Friday would take a battering from opposing defenders, who with no exaggeration in some cases resorted to taking turns to foul him so they could share the bookings out among the defence and avoid a sending off. He would get up and come back for more, physically unaffected, although sometimes retaliating and getting sent-off himself – a real 'result' for the opposition. He famously kissed a policeman after scoring the only goal against Rochdale, and team-mates say his mere presence was often enough to make the difference. Without Robin Friday, there would have been no promotion that season.

Tommy Youlden looks back on that team full of admiration for the way Hurley built a promotion-winning side for next to nothing: 'You look at the team he built up. I came down here for about £5,000, Robin cost next to nothing, he got Dave Moreline who was ex-Fulham and a very good left-back. Added to what we had already, he put together a very good team.' The regular defence consisted of Moreline at left-back, Peters at right-back and centre-halves Geoff Barker and Youlden, with Stuart Henderson playing in a range of positions across the back and defensive midfield and Steve Hetzke replacing the injured Barker towards the end. Peters was signed from non-league Guildford, Barker from perennial lower-division side Darlington. Youlden was a member of the same Arsenal youth setup as Gordon Cumming and arrived at Reading from Portsmouth. Henderson arrived from Brighton & Hove Albion, and was another former First Division apprentice, having been with Chelsea in the mid-1960s, again without ever making the first team.

Cumming and Dunphy were regulars in midfield, with important contributions from Bruce Stuckey and, in the run-in, Bryan Carnaby. Dunphy was an eye-catching signing, having been a regular at Second Division Millwall for eight years, although now in the twilight of his career, signed by his old Eire team-mate for his big-match experience and know-how.

Up front with Friday were Ray Hiron and John Murray. The vastly experienced veteran Hiron had been released by Portsmouth after an 11-year career in which he scored 110 goals in 330 appearances and went on to play 92 times for Reading. Murray was another of Charlie Hurley's 'projects' – a player who had been sacked by his previous club Bury after resolving an altercation with his manager by thumping him. Murray was a key member of the promotion-winning side, scoring 15 times in 40 appearances, but shared Death's lack of enthusiasm for training. He too had flirted with the top level and had short spells in the First Division early in his career with Burnley and Blackpool.

The core of the team was made up of just 16 players, with injuries the main reason for any changes and a few young and fringe players giving enough competition to keep the rest on their toes.

Reading spent the season in and around the promotion places, eventually finishing third, 14 points behind the young Graham Taylor's Lincoln City who took the division by storm, scoring 111 goals using his long-ball philosophy that ultimately earned him his phenomenally successful partnership with Elton John at Watford.

Several factors made this season such a seminal one for success-starved Reading supporters. Firstly, of course, Robin Friday. Secondly, the fact that Reading had never looked like winning a thing for decades, and few believed that they ever would – to the extent that a popular view was that the board actively discouraged success for fear that it would prove too expensive to sustain it. Thirdly, Eamon Dunphy's *Evening Post* column, which brought fans inside the team's trials and tribulations in a way that had never been done before. Dunphy gave us his raw reactions to defeats and described the professional satisfaction of a job well done in victory and used humour and little 'inside' details to give us a feeling that we somehow knew the players as people.

His columns also enabled him to raise issues directly with his readers in a way that most players couldn't. In one article he directly confronted the 'boo-boys' who criticised an individual player and sang the funeral march in a tight home game against Huddersfield. Reading won 1-0, and Dunphy asked,

'What provokes such unbelievable behaviour?' His answer was the years of underachievement the club had gone through, leading fans to react to every disappointment as if it heralded the 'big slide' and the dashing of all their hopes. 'We've got a hell of a chance of winning promotion this season,' he wrote, 'but to get there we need genuine support.'

This is not a specific 'Reading disease' of course, but a manifestation of the psyche of the average supporter, for whom every opposition attack is going to end up with a goal, and every missed chance at the other end is only to be expected, along with biased referees and the fates conspiring against you.

This was another season of understated excellence from the Reading goalkeeper. 'Death was a very, very good keeper,' Dunphy told Roger Titford in his fascinating book *More Than a Job?* which is based on the 1975/76 promotion season. 'Robbed of his desserts by the perception, or rather the reality, of him being small. One of the best keepers I've ever played with, a terrific presence who gave a great sense of calm about him. Very honourable, very straight, very hot-tempered but kept it bottled up. A forbidding man, he took shit from no one.'

Someone he didn't take shit from was Dunphy himself – a man who clearly saw his role as the senior professional, with the experience and credibility to back up his opinions, which of course were always right. In one dressing room encounter, Dunphy was shouting the odds after a game, tearing into his team-mates about what he thought they should or shouldn't be doing differently. This was a regular occurrence and, says Tommy Youlden, some players would be upset by this, while others would get angry. Characteristically, Death waited until Dunphy paused for breath, then quietly said, 'You know what Eamon, the way you're going on you should apply for a job at Mothercare – you'd be a good model for them.' Silence from Dunphy, laughter from Youlden; two players who proved the Brian Clough mantra 'I don't have to love him, I just have to be able to work with him'.

Death limited opposition teams to just over a goal a game, and Reading's third-placed finish and promotion was his first senior team honour as a professional. He played 32 times until a serious injury in a home match against Hartlepool. Challenging for a high ball, Death got a blow in the face. The injury was acutely painful but in those days with only one substitute per team there was no one to take over in goal. Death's extremely high pain threshold meant that he not only completed the game but also played in the next match away at fellow promotion-chasers Huddersfield Town. Form and fitness finally deserted him in Yorkshire, in a calamitous game for the team in every department. The entire defence was spectacularly off-form, and David Dibben's match report in the *Evening Post* pulled no punches after a 3-0 defeat. This was a fourth consecutive away loss, and the nagging sense of impending doom and the legacy of 50 years of failure loomed large once again among the Reading faithful.

Death played badly and was described by Dibben in his match report as being 'all at sea' along with his entire defence, 'losing track' of crosses and 'leaping off his line and completely missing his punch' to concede the third. Unknown to the team, the crowd, and presumably to the manager, Death was struggling with what Dibben described as 'a serious facial injury'. This injury was the legacy of the collision in the previous game, which had broken his jaw.

Death was out for the final 14 matches, giving reserve keeper John Turner an extremely rare run in the team. Turner did a fine job, seeing them through a nerve-jangling run-in to clinch promotion, and was equally parsimonious towards opposing forwards.

It was Turner who played in the home game against Tranmere Rovers on 31 March 1976. As Dunphy wrote in his column before the match – a long poem about the promotion run-in – 'The world reduced to just three teams; Tranmere, Reading, and Huddersfield.' Three teams were fighting for the last two promotion places, Northampton Town having joined Lincoln City in an unreachable top two by that stage of the season. Before the match the teams were level on points with Tranmere third and Reading fourth on goal average. It would be impossible to overstate the importance of the occasion to both sides, so it was therefore the ultimate test for nervous Royals fans fearing another in a long line of bitter disappointments in their quest to escape from the Fourth Division.

LIFE IN THE BASEMENT

If Reading's players shared those nerves they hid them well, destroying their nearest rivals 5-0, with John Murray scoring a hat-trick including two penalties, and Robin Friday scoring two. Reading's third goal has passed into legend as the best goal anyone there has ever seen. With no TV footage this moment of magic was witnessed by just over 11,000 people and is cherished all the more for that.

Everyone there has their own version of the goal, so I will give you mine. Friday was 35 yards from goal, out towards the left touchline, when he took a long ball from defence. With his back to goal and a Tranmere defender breathing down his neck, he took the ball on his right instep, flicking it over his head and sending the defender the wrong way. In one movement he turned and volleyed it high into the top corner of the Tranmere net, then wheeled away in triumph. The by now bemused and defeated away team stood as if rooted to the spot as his team-mates and adoring public experienced one of the best moments of their collective lives.

Of course it's easy to romanticise; after all, this was a Fourth Division striker scoring in a battle for third place and promotion.

If it helps to put things into perspective for readers who weren't there, or who never saw Friday play, there is a picture of the moment with referee Clive Thomas standing among the wreckage of the Tranmere team with his hands on his head in disbelief. Thomas turned to Friday and said that was the best goal he had ever seen, to which Friday replied, 'You should come here more often. I do that every week.'

Thomas was the most well-known Football League referee of the era, had refereed at World Cups and shared a pitch with the world's greatest players. Here is his assessment of Friday's 'wonder goal': 'Even up against the likes of Pelé and Cruyff that rates as the best goal I have ever seen.'

Playing with Death

John Turner (1975-77)

As a promising young goalkeeper, Turner spent three years at Derby County under Brian Clough, who called him 'Young John' and made him his first loan signing on taking over as manager of Brighton & Hove Albion. Charlie Hurley signed him for Reading in 1975 and he played 31 times for the club, his appearances limited by the consistent excellence of the regular goalkeeper. On leaving Reading, he had a long and distinguished career with Torquay, Chesterfield and Peterborough United, playing a total of 338 games.

He was player of the year nearly every bloody year, wasn't he?

Deathy was so laid-back. When I got married I got a club flat on Tilehurst Road, next to Friday, Deathy, Alan Lewis and Dennis Nelson for a fiver a week. Great it was. We were good friends, we used to walk to the club together.

TINY KEEPER

He knew I was after his place but there was no animosity. He was always confident. I wanted to take his place, but I respected him. I used to say to him, 'One day Deathy I'm going to have your place.' He would just smile. Once when he was having a bit of a bad time, he said to me, 'You might be getting your chance soon.' When I did get my chance, he just shook my hand and wished me good luck. That season was the only time I won promotion in all my life.

He kept goal like Gordon Banks; he was cool, never flustered. If he got smashed he just got up and got on with it. He had a good pair of hands and made the ball stick. He was tactically perfect, his positioning was perfect, he was cool, didn't panic, had soft hands. He would catch it most of the time and only occasionally would he punch it. His timing was immaculate. He had a good spring on him. He was athletic – how is beyond me because he never worked at it. In training he would just kick them out, head them out, he wouldn't dive.

If he'd been six feet tall he would have played for England and he would never have been allowed to leave West Ham.

Like all goalkeepers we always think we can play five-a-side, and he always enjoyed those games – the only bit of training he was ever enthusiastic about. The only time we talked goalkeeping would be on the coach or sometimes during goalkeeping training. He didn't wear gloves; didn't like them.

He was a scruffy bugger - if you gave him a £500 suit he would still look like a tramp! He had his greyhounds, he used to like a trip to the bookies. He used to go home to his family after matches. He had this thick mop of black hair and didn't dress up at all. If you ever saw him in the street, you wouldn't think he was a footballer.

I can still see the picture of him sitting in the dressing room with legs crossed, sitting next to a lad called Wayne Wanklyn. There was a pack of 20 Embassy on the shelf above him, and I look at those and think 'that's what killed him'. He was only 54.

I came to Reading from Derby County in 1975 - I'd just got back from a tour in Africa. Dave Mackay said another club was in for me. When I found out it was Reading and Charlie Hurley, who was a hero because I'm a Sunderland boy, of course I was going to sign. He picked me up in his Capri, took me to Elm Park and I signed for him. I was the youngest in the squad and the dressing room was full of senior pros like Eamon Dunphy, Ray Hiron, Tommy Youlden and Geoff Barker who had been through the mill and seen it and done it.

I was the first ever player Cloughie signed when he went to Brighton. Dave Mackay had taken over as Derby manager. He said, 'Cloughie's in for you, he wants you to go to Brighton.' Cloughie just burst into his old office in front of the new manager and said, 'Young John, come with me.' We got into his Merc that I used to wash when I was an apprentice, he drove me to the park and asked me if I wanted to go to Brighton. I said yes. He asked me how much I was on. I said, 'Don't you know? You were the manager!' He said, 'I don't know what any of you boys are on – I don't even know what Roy McFarland was on!' I said, 'I'm on £40 a week.' He said, 'I'll pay you £60.' He offered me £15 a week expenses and told me I was to go home every weekend to see my parents. I said, 'I don't want to go home every weekend; I want to be playing football!' 'You daft bugger,' he said. 'You're not going home, that £15 a week is for you!' It was a loan deal, and I never played a single game at Brighton because Cloughie left straight away for Leeds.

Reading was my stepping stone into league football. I used to do part-time work for Roy Tranter's Thames Valley Cleaning Company. In the hot summer I got a job hod-carrying and was on much more money as a hod-carrier than I was as a professional footballer. But they were great times, I absolutely loved it.

Dave Moreline (1974-81)
Signed from Fulham in 1974 by Charlie Hurley, Moreline brought some much-needed higher division experience

to Elm Park when the manager was putting together a team capable of gaining promotion from the Fourth Division. A cultured left-back described by team-mate John Turner as 'the Bobby Moore of the lower divisions', he went on to make 166 appearances for Reading before retiring in 1981.

The first time I met him I recognised him from his days at West Ham. He walked into the dressing room unshaven and under one arm he had a copy of *Sporting Life* and in the other hand he had 20 Embassy, and I thought, 'This lad will do for me.'

Steve was a very quiet lad and very unassuming. After matches he would just disappear; while I would go out with Murray and a few others Steve would go straight home to his wife. There were four of us who lived in flats in Tilehurst Road: Steve, John Murray underneath him and just along the road was me and next door to me was Robin Friday. We used to pay the grand sum of £5 per month to the club in rent. I remember Robin painted his ceiling black with stars on it. Before games we used to have Robin over for breakfast. He was a real chameleon; he was polite and nice as pie with my wife and you wouldn't think it was the same person who would be out with the lads later.

Pre-season we used to go on these long runs to get us into condition and before one of these Steve tried to influence Charlie by saying, 'Boss, you wouldn't expect a Derby winner to run in the Grand National would you?' intimating that he and I were sprinters rather than marathon runners. I remember one hot July day we were running past a pub called the Cunning Man in Burghfield, and we were at the back as usual, just trying to do our job as best we could. We were ambling along next to the river and Steve suddenly stopped and bent down next to me. I thought he was pulling his socks up but instead he pulled out a packet of Embassy. I thought that's a good idea and we ended up sitting by the river for a while with our socks off and our feet in the water having a little smoke before we carried on.

At half-time he would have a smoke during the half-time talk. Pre-match meal would be a full English breakfast and then out you'd go and play. Charlie's team talks were very straightforward, telling us to go out and play and to 'let them know you're there' in the first tackle.

Loved his horseracing, loved his greyhounds, loved his golf. After I left Reading, I used to meet up with him at Calcot golf course. We weren't very good but we enjoyed it!

I can never remember him having a go at defenders. He wasn't a [Peter] Schmeichel shouting at people, he would just quietly do his job, put his clothes on and go home.

He was happy, he never complained, as long as he had his *Sporting Life* and his fags he was happy.

When I think of him as a goalkeeper it was just a feeling of complete confidence; he knew his job, I knew mine and each of us knew what the other would do. I think that back five unit was an important reason why we got promoted in 1975/76.

At Christmas we all used to get a turkey from the club, but Charlie decided that because Robin Friday always dressed in his crocodile boots, T-shirt and jackets that he would buy him a nice warm jumper instead. Robin wasn't too pleased about that. When he turned up at the next game dressed in his usual style, Charlie asked him where the jumper was. 'Oh,' said Robin, 'I took it down to Reading market and swapped it for a turkey.' Managing Robin was a difficult task, but Charlie did a great job with him.

On a Friday before a game we would play five-a-side on this car park outside Elm Park which was made of asphalt and surrounded by rusty old wire fences with jagged bits sticking out. Steve loved five-a-side and would tear around the pitch like a little terrier kicking seven bells out of us. The ball would disappear over the fence and land in people's gardens and Steve would climb fences and go and get the ball back – it was like being back at school.

Travelling with or near the team was not always easy for the press and others. I remember the *Evening Post*'s David Dibben stopped travelling with the team after Robin Friday sneaked into his room and shaved his toothbrush with a razor.

I used to room with Steve and we would stay in these hotels up north. We would watch a bit of TV and try to relax before getting some sleep and people would be leaving the hotel bar and making a lot of noise. Steve would lean out of our fifth-floor window and tip a glass of water over their heads. We would hear them shout, 'Who the hell did that?' and I was saying to him, don't do that, they'll come up and find us. 'They won't find us,' he said, 'they have no idea which room we're in.' Then he calmly sat back down with his *Sporting Life*.

We were playing in a charity match at Cold Ash near Newbury, and one of the Showbiz Eleven was the tallest man in Britain. I was in the bar and Steve came in on the shoulders of this 7ft 8in man, pretending to be a jockey on the back of this giant horse, whipping him with his right hand and shouting, 'Come on son, come on!'

Gary Peters (1975-79 and 1985-88)

An overlapping right-back blessed with pace and power, Peters played 256 games for Reading in two separate spells. In his first spell, he was an integral part of two promotion-winning teams and after returning he played in the record-breaking sequence of 13 wins from the start of a season as Reading won the Third Division championship. In between, Peters played for Wimbledon as they won promotion from the Fourth Division and captained them to promotion from the Third Division. He went into management after playing, with Preston North End (where he signed one David Beckham on loan), Exeter City and Shrewsbury Town. In addition to his fine playing record, Peters can lay claim to an important part in Reading folklore as the man whose long, cross-field pass was flicked up and volleyed home by Robin Friday against Tranmere.

That year, 1975, when I joined Reading was an unbelievable year. Steve's level at that time was outstanding. Robin Friday was there and he was incredible and produced so much history for the club. Steve lived in virtually the same house as Robin, as any player signed by the club who needed somewhere to live was given a space in the three storeys of flats by the ground. Steve was such a nice fella but no one would say anything out of order to him. He was so tough mentally.

He wasn't the biggest goalkeeper but he was brilliant, and no one would think that if he was fit anyone else would play in goal. Charlie Hurley had put the team together, and the same team would play most weeks. He just made us do the same things every time, and everyone had to do what they had to do except for Robin Friday who just did whatever he liked and the rest of us had to cover for him.

Out of all the people there, everyone gave so much respect to Steve Death for the way he handled himself as the goalkeeper. Steve wasn't as big a character as Robin but was equally as strong. Even Robin looked up to Steve because of the way he handled himself. He was the friendliest, most respected person at the football club.

Everyone who's been at Reading talks about Robin Friday but Steve sticks out to me as a legend because he was there so long doing the thing he loved and was so brilliant at doing it. I don't think you'll find any player who has a bad word to say about him. He was such a special character.

He was such a good goalkeeper, and I don't think I've played with a better one. I played with Joe Hart at Shrewsbury who went on to play for England, and with

Dave Beasant at Wimbledon, but Steve was the best I've ever played with.

There was so much experience in that team with Ray Hiron, Eamon Dunphy, John Murray and Gordon Cumming and once that team got going you weren't going to beat it. After a game everyone had a drink together and stayed together and there was a feeling of being part of something.

Steve was quiet, he would be sat in the changing rooms, but he would make sure that things were done in the right way. Steve was so friendly, and that's why some people might have thought he wasn't tough, but he was tough because he'd get it right all the time. He wouldn't have a go at you but you'd think 'I've let him down', because people had so much respect for him.

It wasn't the noise he made or how much he said, because he didn't need to. In many ways you felt as if he was in charge, even though he hardly said anything. It was left to people like Eamon Dunphy to do the talking. The rest of the team, and there were so many experienced players, knew what they had behind them and they respected him for it. I was much younger than them and I learned so much from them all. If there was going to be any drama it would be in front of me, never behind me! He was solid as a rock.

TINY KEEPER

I never saw him fall out with anybody in the four years I was there with him. He had a 'take your breath away' ability as a goalkeeper and had a great effect on the rest of the team. He was part of the club and because he lived across the road you could go and see him at any time. He was always there and always ready with a smile and would be happy to have a chat. You just wouldn't want to be without him. John Turner came in as reserve keeper – he was a decent goalkeeper but the only time he ever got a game was if Steve was injured.

To be 5ft 7.5in and be in professional football you had to be tough. If you step out of line or say the wrong thing someone's going to sort it out, but he had everybody's respect so much that no one would dream of saying the wrong thing to him. You wouldn't want to have a row with him. He was physically tough, you wouldn't see him hurt, he would come and get every ball and take the pressure off the players. He saved me a few times!

4

A Load of Old Bull

*How Reading snatched defeat
from the jaws of victory*

THE LONG, hot summer of 1976 saw Britain facing hosepipe bans and the Labour government appointing former Football League referee Denis Howell as minister for drought as the football calendar ticked around from 1975/76 to 1976/77. In those days the close-season seemed as endless as the heatwave, with almost four months between the last game of the previous campaign and the first of the new. Four months in which players and fans of every team are entitled to reflect on the last campaign and dream that the next season will be 'our year'.

For Reading supporters, as well as the long-awaited promotion with its memories of Tranmere Rovers and home form which saw only one defeat in 23, there was special cause for optimism. All the players who had achieved so much were still there, along with the manager and his assistant; a couple of new signings and they could establish themselves among the better teams in the league and maybe, just maybe, aim for the promised land of the Second Division. So, what did they do? They got relegated instead.

The first sign that something was wrong came before a ball had been kicked. My sister and her friend were among a small knot of Reading fans waiting near the ground for the supporters' club coach to take them to Gillingham for the first match of the season. She describes their shock at seeing a small, scruffily dressed figure walking past them with his dog. It was their star goalkeeper, and he had no intention of joining his fellow players on the team coach to Kent. Steve Death had been a fixture in the team since 1969 and when he was fit, he played. This was not a good sign.

Instead of using the summer to build on the team's success and invest, however cautiously, in the future, Reading's hierarchy did just about everything they could to stop their progress in its tracks. In the weeks after clinching third spot and achieving their goal for the season, everyone waited for news of some kind of reward in their pay packets. Not a word was heard from anyone in the club's leadership. Effectively, as manager, Charlie Hurley was being hung out to dry with no influence and no information. Not only could he not sign anyone, he couldn't even tell his own players what their future held.

One scarcely believable story is symptomatic of the state of relations within the club at this time. A local butcher had promised that if Reading won promotion he would buy a bull and give all the meat to the players. With the salary levels of players at the time this was a significant benefit, and the squad were looking forward to taking home some prime steak for their families. Following promotion, the butcher made good on his promise and invited the players to the stockyard and advised them on the best animal to buy. The meat was then packaged and delivered to the club, which is where the drama unfolded as by the time the players arrived to pick up their spoils the best cuts of meat had disappeared, leaving what some described as 'bags of offal'.

The *Evening Post* ran a story speculating on where all the fillet steak had gone, and who had taken all the sirloin. The direct implication was that all the best cuts had gone to the manager and directors. This was a huge embarrassment for the management at the club and Tommy Youlden remembers how it was received by them, 'Charlie called us all in, went apeshit and spelt out exactly what he would do if he ever found out who leaked the story to the press.' Eamon Dunphy included the story in his autobiography many years later, so it still clearly rankled as an example of how little the players were valued by the board of directors.

Throughout that summer it dawned on all the players that they were clearly not going to be rewarded for their efforts with a bonus or pay rise of any kind, and the reservoirs of goodwill among the playing staff at Reading evaporated along with those of the Thames Water Board.

True to form, Dunphy didn't take the situation lying down. Along with a small group of senior players including Steve Death, John Murray and Gordon Cumming, he held out for what they saw as a fair deal.

Dave Moreline, a key defender in that promotion-winning side, remembers the breakdown in the relationship between club and players clearly, 'My first pay packet at Reading was £45 per week and it didn't really seem as if it was likely to go up after promotion. Eamon worked out that the crowds would be bigger and how much money that would bring in, and that we could then reasonably ask for more money in the Third Division. There was this big meeting with all of us and Frank Waller, the chairman. We were prepared for it with our wage demands and Dunphy gave a speech with all his facts and figures. I think we even threatened to strike if we didn't get a better wage offer after promotion. Frank Waller got up and said quietly to Dunphy and the rest of us, "That's interesting, but there will be a Reading side put out in the first game of the season. We'll find players and we'll play them." So we all crept away with our tails between our legs and agreed our own wages individually.'

The beleaguered Hurley tried in vain to stem the tide of dissatisfaction but instead saw it turn into open revolt. He even tried to resolve things with some old-fashioned 'divide and rule' tactics, offering the rebel group of senior players an extra fiver a week if they would accept their new terms and call off the dispute, knowing that the rest of the squad would then be likely to fall into line. They refused, only signing in the end to avoid the risk of being automatically employed on the same terms as last season, with no pay increase at all.

One by one their patience snapped. Geoff Barker, a salt-of-the-earth centre-half, temporarily gave up football altogether at the age of 27 and went back home to manage the family undertaking business, before briefly being persuaded to come back a few months later. Dunphy further angered the club hierarchy by writing a scathing *Evening Post* column that week, including the barbed comment that 'Geoff was dependable and, it seems, expendable'.

Youlden put himself on the transfer list while Hurley was away on a family holiday in the close-season, with the upset manager demanding to know why Tommy hadn't waited for him to get back to work. Halfway through the new season, Youlden was gone. John Murray was made available for transfer. Dunphy was transfer-listed at the board's behest, with no argument from Hurley whose patience with the belligerent Irishman had long worn thin, although he did eventually stay and complete the season – his last as a professional footballer in England.

Disaster was finally confirmed in late December, when the board's Christmas present to Reading players and supporters was the sale of Robin Friday to Second Division Cardiff City for a knockdown fee of £30,000. In truth, there was little choice for anyone involved as Friday had become increasingly impossible to manage and the board wanted to cash in on their prized asset before he also became impossible to sell. Friday's parting shot was to tell the local press, 'There doesn't seem to be any ambition at the club. If you ask me, they would be happy enough to stroll on in the bottom half of the Third Division forever.'

The move ended disastrously for all parties though as Friday, far from home and out of control, introduced himself on debut against a star-studded Fulham side by squeezing Bobby Moore's testicles, scoring twice and having a third attempt cleared off the line. That was as good as it got for Friday at Cardiff, where he briefly dazzled before he began being late for training or missing it completely; when he did show up his erratic and at times violent behaviour in training and in games led to a permanent rift with his new manager and by December of the following season he had left the game altogether.

Hurley didn't last much longer than half his team, dramatically walking out of the dressing room at half-time during an abysmal performance at home to Bury in February 1977. Announcing 'I've had enough of this', he turned to assistant manager Maurice Evans and said, 'It's all yours Maurice,' then turned on his heels and left the ground. This remains the first and only time a manager has quit his job *during* a match and testifies to the intolerable amount of stress he was under at the time, as well as his combustible nature. Walking out cost Hurley his job, his severance pay and any future position in football. All this a few short months after masterminding his club's first promotion in 50 years. A sad end for a legendary player who did his level best to deliver as manager for his parsimonious employer.

Roger Ware was covering the match for the local paper, and remembers, 'Charlie was enduring a torrid time from the fans after such a long run without a win, which had begun in December. This was the 11th match in that run and our "bogey team" Bury were the opponents. That was all it needed – and by half-time Reading were losing 3-0. Almost immediately after the teams disappeared down the tunnel at half-time, Reading re-appeared, skipper Eamon Dunphy leading them out for a pow-wow in the centre-circle.

'Clearly something was wrong – and that "something" was apparently Charlie offering to re-arrange the features of one or two players he considered had let him, and the team, down. He packed it in there and then.

'The alleged threat to offer a bloody nose or two was utterly out of character with Charlie, who I considered – and still do – one of the most decent and amiable people I have ever met.'

Dave Moreline also speaks highly of Hurley and his impact on the culture and performances at Reading but knows that he was working in a difficult environment and that he was clearly affected by it towards the end: 'Charlie was good to play for. He was a complete change from my previous boss at Fulham, Alec Stock. There was nothing technical, he just said go out and play hard. It was the traditional "let them know you're there" in the first tackle. He frightened some of the players by telling us not to worry if we broke our legs because we have the best doctors in town, which led to some thinking, "I'm not doing that!" Charlie would talk to you man to man and if he thought you were a prat he would tell you to your face. I remember when he dropped me once, he phoned me at home and told me why, which I thought was a fair thing to do.

'Sadly, during that season after promotion Charlie came to think that there was a conspiracy against him and that we weren't giving our all as players for him any more. Nothing could have been further from the truth. Once that little spell of dispute over wages was over for me that was that and we just carried on trying to give our best. It wasn't good enough, but we were definitely trying. Against Bury we came in at half-time and Maurice said to us, "The boss has gone!"'

John Turner, who had joined Reading in part because Charlie Hurley had been a hero for him as a Sunderland-obsessed boy, was sad to see his manager go, but he had some touching proof Charlie hadn't forgotten him. 'Charlie wrote me a letter when he left. He said, "Get on with your life John, and use that height and strength you've got." I still have that letter.'

Gordon Cumming, however, gives a brutal summary of the mindset of the professional footballer, even at the moment of their greatest achievements: 'When a team gets promoted, the manager thinks he got the players promoted and they should be grateful. The players think they got the manager promoted and they should be rewarded.'

No wonder Friday had turned to Dunphy soon after the high of promotion and commented, 'It doesn't last long, does it?'

Even during the promotion year Reading rarely stayed over for away games. They would leave early in the morning, stop at a motorway services for lunch or at a chip shop on the way home, and disgorge the team late at night to make their way home. There was a £1 limit on what could be spent on each player's food and anyone exceeding their allowance would have to pay for it themselves.

On one occasion this led to a tirade of abuse from Eamon Dunphy towards his manager on the team coach, in which Dunphy advised Hurley of the stupidity of treating professional athletes in this way and expecting a performance out of them at the end of it. Hurley sat and took it in silence, then promptly dropped Dunphy from the team. John Turner delivered a succinct judgement on the team's unofficial shop steward. 'Dunphy was a horrible skinny little fucker,' he says. 'He had a bad mouth, but he did speak the truth!'

Tommy Youlden has another example of the club's attitude towards its key employees. 'One season,' he told me, 'I played the first four or five games and then got an Achilles tendon injury and was out for about three-quarters of the season. I had an operation at Farnham Park and went into a private hospital for rehabilitation. I had a room to myself for five or six days but there was nothing in it, so I asked if I could have a TV in the room. I went back to the club afterwards to get back to full fitness using the facilities at Palmer Park, unaware that Hurley had been told there was a real risk that I might never have been able to recover enough for first-team football. When I eventually recovered and was able to play again, the club secretary Fred May called me into his office and told me that I would have to pay for the television set. May told me that the club didn't have insurance cover for the TV in my room, so he was going to have to take it out of my wages.' Youlden's response was unprintable, and the incident has stayed with him to this day, providing a perfect microcosm of the priorities of life under the regime at the club in the mid-1970s.

This was the background to the start of the 1976/77 season, and the reason Steve Death, still in dispute over wages, woke up on the first day of the new campaign and chose to walk his dogs rather than board the coach for Gillingham with his team-mates. John Turner was injured and Death was the only available goalkeeper.

David Downs, club historian, journalist, author and expert in all things Reading, was travelling to the match with *Evening Post* reporter David Dibben. They had seen Death leaving the newsagents in Norfolk Road opposite the ground and heard that he had gone back to his club flat. They had also heard that the injured Turner had been seen limping on to the team coach. Dibben, ever the reporter, sensed a story and both men were concerned for Death and the team, so Dibben suggested that they call on him to find out what was going on.

Downs recalls, 'We went round to Deathy's house and found that he had gone back to bed with the latest copy of *Sporting Life*, with his pet dog lying on the bed with him. Roy Tranter, a club director, had already been in and tried to persuade him to play and David now put in his two penn'orth. Dibben pointed out that if he didn't play he would only get fined and lose even more money. The risk of losing two weeks' wages was enough to convince him and eventually, Deathy agreed and said, "All right, I'll play, but how am I going to get there?" Dave said, "I'll drive you." So we waited while Deathy had a quick wash and brush up, got changed and had a piece of toast, then we called in to see Fred May to tell him what we were doing. Fred phoned ahead to leave a message for Charlie Hurley, and we then raced off at breakneck speed to catch up with the team where they were having lunch in Gillingham.

'Deathy sat in the front with Dibben and I sat in the back. If Deathy smoked one cigarette on the journey he must have smoked ten, while he criticised the management of the club in no uncertain terms. We finally met up with the team, handed him over to Charlie Hurley and he went straight to the ground and of course played the proverbial blinder. After the game I went into the press conference where Gillingham manager Gerry Summers turned to Dave and I and said, "If it wasn't for you two we would have won that game!" because Steve played so well in a 2-2 draw.'

Hurley kept Death in the team despite this episode, showing once again how valuable he was to his managers. In discussing him with Downs, Hurley gave his goalkeeper what can only be described as the most backhanded of compliments, describing him as 'too dim to feel any fear' as he threw himself at the feet of opposing centre-forwards. He went on to play 42 times in what turned out to be an awful season in which Reading were relegated with just 35 points, conceding 73 goals in the process and scoring only 49. The team went 12 games without a win from the end of December to the beginning of March, and lost more than half of their matches, including 16 away defeats.

As Dunphy told Roger Titford in *More Than a Job?*, 'Once you've been shabbily treated by a club it breaks that nebulous camaraderie that sustains you in tough games, or when you go behind. It becomes impossible to be successful then.'

John Turner, who played in the run-in to the promotion season, is another player with a tale of meanness and misrepresentation, and another to leave by the end of this miserable and anti-climactic campaign: 'I left at the end of the relegation season. When we won promotion I signed a blind contract – Charlie told me not to worry because everything would be filled in for me. Instead, they gave me a rise but took away my loyalty bonus so I ended up even, with no pay rise. Torquay came in for me and I took the move and had to go to a tribunal.

'When we were walking into the hearing, Frank O'Farrell was with me, and Roy Bentley was there for Reading, having taken over from Fred May as club secretary. Frank looked at Roy, and Roy said to him, "I'm sorry. This would never have happened if I'd been secretary. I'm going to tell the truth." The blind contract had been arranged by the previous club secretary and Bentley couldn't bring himself to defend it. So, when I got into the room with Alan Hardaker, Ted Croker and all the FA bigwigs, I told my story exactly as it had happened. Torquay had already offered £15,000 for me, but a few weeks later I was running around the track at the ground and Frank showed me a letter setting the fee at £3,000. I had just moved into my house and had no carpets, so the club bought me carpets because they'd saved so much money on my fee!'

Tommy Youlden is in no doubt that the directors caused most of the problems for the club at that time. 'The thing that held Reading back was the board of directors. A few years later Frank Waller tried to merge the club with Oxford through a secret deal with Robert Maxwell, which says a lot about the way they thought. I got on well with Charlie, but the board of directors, dear oh dear. The secretary was Fred May, who pulled the purse strings. He did everything the directors asked him to do, but to think of him being in charge of a football club, well! Charlie couldn't spend any money, couldn't sign the players he wanted to. The way it was handled after we won promotion, even days after we won it, was dreadful. I went in to see Fred before I made my decision to leave, and I wasn't at all happy with what he had to say. I left Reading for Aldershot in the Fourth Division and they paid me much more than I was ever paid at Reading.

'Charlie went to work for his brother-in-law's business as a salesman in a packaging company and I think he always regretted leaving so impulsively, and perhaps he also regretted that he hadn't been able to take the Sheffield United job when it was offered early on in the promotion season as it would have taken him back into the Second Division.'

With Hurley gone the manager's chalice, tarnished if not quite poisoned after the events of the past six months, did indeed pass to his assistant manager, Maurice Evans. Evans was a Reading man through and through, having joined the ground staff in 1952 at the age of 16, and played with distinction for the club at right-half for 459 matches. During all those appearances, Evans was never booked, and he is spoken of by everyone who knew him as a genuine and lovely man. He left Reading in 1967 to go into coaching and management, returning in 1974 as Hurley's assistant. Many players give him a lot of the credit for the way the Reading team of 1975/76 was tactically set up.

Youlden says, 'I had a lot of respect for Maurice Evans. Charlie had poached him to be the coach. He had a lot of success. He was a gentleman. When Charlie left, Maurice became manager and had promotions with Reading and went on to have success with Oxford, winning the Milk [Football League] Cup with them. He had a lot of input with the way we played in that promotion team with Charlie, a lot of influence. He wasn't outspoken or controversial, but he knew the game. He put some good teams together and had a tremendous amount of success. He never bawled and shouted. He joined the year before we were promoted and had a lot of input.'

By the time Evans took over after Hurley's half-time exit against Bury, it was too late for him to save Reading's Third Division status, which in the words of the old joke had lasted for exactly three seasons – autumn, winter and spring. If he were to rebuild the team, he would have to start all over again, back in the Fourth Division.

Playing with Death

Tommy Youlden (1972-77)

Like Gordon Cumming, centre-half Tommy Youlden was another product of the Arsenal youth system, signing for Reading from Portsmouth in 1972. His 163 appearances included being part of the 1975/76 promotion side along with the likes of Eamon Dunphy, Steve Death, John Murray and Robin Friday. He was part of the exodus in the ill-fated 1976/77 season following promotion, joining local rivals Aldershot, and later went to Chelsea as youth team coach.

Steve was here when I arrived and a lot longer after I left. He must have won the player of the year award on two or three occasions while I was there. There were a few First Division clubs who came to watch him but no one made an offer. This can only have been because of his height and stature, because as far as a shot-stopper and his talent as a goalkeeper there could have been nothing else; I just think managers were obsessed by their own ideas of what a goalkeeper should look like and had made up their minds in advance. He was an outstanding goalkeeper.

He was very easy-going. He never said very much in the changing room but when he did say something he was quite funny. He was a very unassuming guy. He would sit and get changed and go out and play, and after the game he would go home. He would do his job and he was reliable. I had a lot of time for him, a lot of respect for him. He was exceptional. Man United players used to say that if somebody got through they knew that [Peter] Schmeichel would stop them, and we felt the same about Steve. You knew that if somebody got through and he was the last line of defence, if it was a one-to-one Steve would come out on top. He never caused any trouble in the dressing room. No bravado, very quiet. If you met him in a bar or somewhere you wouldn't think he was a professional footballer but when he got on the pitch you knew you would get a performance from him. I had a lot of time for him, and you knew when you got out there Steve would be there for you, which was important for me as a centre-half.

He was a very unassuming guy in the dressing room, a terrific guy to have in the dressing room with you. I had a lot of time for him. He did like a smoke, that was his only trouble, but he was a character, no doubt whatsoever.

Having played with him week after week I can honestly say his size was never an issue. I just thought of him as an outstanding keeper. Does he save shots? Yes. Does he concede many goals? No. Is he good on one-to-ones? Yes. Is he good in the air? Yes. But when scouts came to watch him they had this fixed idea of what a goalkeeper should look like. When I think about it now, watching the current England goalkeeper, he's not very big but he's outstanding, and he reminds me of Steve.

Gillingham away. We left for Gillingham and Steve never turned up. 'Where's Deathy?' David Dibben phoned Steve up and asked him why he wasn't going. He then drove over to his house and picked him up. We had a stop at the services for a pre-match meal and Deathy was there. We had no idea why until much later. Just think of the sports reporter from your local paper driving your keeper to meet the first team. Steve would never have done something as controversial as that unless it was something serious, but the board were penny-pinching and wouldn't invest in the football club at all.

Roy Tranter, who was one of the directors, went to visit Steve in hospital. He was seriously ill by that time.

Steve said to him, 'Do us a favour, give us a fag.' Right to the very end, he was always the same guy, he was never going to be any different.

Lawrie Sanchez (1977-84)

Famously signed by Maurice Evans while still at school in the town's Presentation College, Sanchez juggled studying for a degree in management science while playing professionally as an 18-year-old. His first season ended with winning the Fourth Division title while Steve Death and the defence set their record of clean sheets. The midfielder played 262 games for Reading before moving to upwardly mobile Wimbledon, famously scoring the only goal as the 'Crazy Gang beat the Culture Club' in the Wimbledon v Liverpool FA Cup Final of 1988. He went on to manage a variety of clubs and had a three-year stint as manager of the Northern Ireland national team.

He was very small. He wouldn't have been a goalkeeper in today's game as keepers have morphed into 6ft 2in minimum; there is no one of 5ft 7.5in playing in the top divisions these days. You've got to be exceptionally good to be a keeper at that height and the thing is, he was exceptionally good. He came out and held crosses which goalkeepers don't do these days – they come out and punch them. He was lucky in that team to have Steve Wood, Steve Hetzke and Martin Hicks in front of him who were dominant in the air.

Shot-stopping, he was second to none and used to pull out saves from nowhere – he was very agile. In training he was the complete opposite. I found shooting practice completely pointless as he hated it. He used to stand in the middle of the goal and if he could put a foot or an elbow out to stop it he would; beyond that he just stood in the goal and didn't bother moving. He would never dive in training, but he came alive on a Saturday. Some people can get away with it and he was one of those that did. He wasn't that fussed.

By the time I got there he was the old man of the team. He loved a fag in the dressing room. They had to go in the toilets to smoke. He was very much of the Robin Friday school of footballers; he turned up and played on a Saturday but the rest of it was just a waste of time. I was never very close to him but I got on with him. He looked a lot older than he was and he wasn't the best dressed in the world either, looked a bit of a scruffy so-and-so most of the time.

He didn't say a lot, but he could say a cutting word when one needed to be said. When he did speak, us young players listened. We had great respect for his goalkeeping. No one doubted his goalkeeping.

PLAYING WITH DEATH

You know with some people they don't have to say anything. As a player if you didn't try in training you would normally get slaughtered by the manager, but no one said anything to Deathy because he did things on a Saturday nobody else could do. You don't go that amount of games without pulling off a great save or two. It's not luck to go that long.

Steve told me he played one game for West Ham and there was a newspaper strike on the Sunday afterwards so there was no report on his performance or how he did.

Amazing - 12 games at the end of one season and into the next. We had that run at the end of the season. It was a tremendous achievement. I was only 19 at the time and I still have the picture of us coming off the pitch after the 3-0 win away at Port Vale that clinched the championship. We beat Grimsby 4-0 at Elm Park and John Alexander scored all four goals; he didn't normally score but he was on fire that day. They were second in the table and we played before 15,000 at Elm Park. After that we just steamrollered people, you don't achieve that kind of record unless your goalkeeper is on tip-top form and he was. We honestly thought we could beat anybody.

I was surprised when he left. He was still a legend - 33 for a goalkeeper isn't that old. Deathy wasn't an athlete in any shape or form but he didn't get injured either. He was one of those players, you would just know on any matchday, 'Deathy's in goal'; other people changed around but Deathy's always in goal. All of a sudden, next season, Ron Fearon was in goal and Deathy was gone. In training we had two goalkeepers who were diving about trying to prove themselves and perhaps Deathy thought I don't want any more of this, these young pups running around.

5

1,103 Minutes

A record-breaking promotion season by those who were there

STEVE DEATH'S legend is built on many things; firstly, on his unusual and memorable name. *Reading Chronicle* reporter Colin Gunney remembers opposition fans and gentlemen of the press at away matches continually mispronouncing it. The most common rendering was Steve De'Ath, with an unnecessary apostrophe and a stress on the last (invented) syllable, which only existed because people wanted to avoid saying the taboo word. Gunney took great pleasure in looking people in the eyes and correcting them by saying, straight-faced and with a hint of menace, 'It's Death,' and going on to assert that this was how the man himself pronounced it. Graham Nickless, who reported on Reading matches in the late 1970s, also remembers people calling him De'Ath and having to correct them, ten years after Steve had signed for the Royals and played more than 400 games. Everywhere he went people noticed the name, either commenting on it or going to great lengths to pretend it was something different.

Secondly, Steve was a famously quiet man who didn't give interviews, so most fans have never heard his voice and would rarely have read any quotes from him in the press. He would turn up, do his job, and go home. As club historian, supporter, author and journalist David Downs told me, 'Steve was just a quiet country lad who had one particular skill, which was playing as a goalkeeper, and that carried him through to his early 30s.' Gordon Cumming, a long-time team-mate of Death, says, 'I used to sit next to Stevie in the changing room for matches but hardly got a word out of him. He would just get up and get on with it. He was a great lad, never any trouble, but very quiet.'

The next aspect of the man that raised his profile in the football world was, of course, his lack of height. This has been commented on by everyone who appears in this book and is cited as the reason why he missed out on a top-flight and even on an international career. Alexandria Death told me that when her mum first met her dad, in a Reading nightclub, she asked him what he did for a living. When Steve told her he was a goalkeeper she just laughed. Alexandria says her dad was very particular about people getting his height exactly right, and when he read or heard himself referred to as being 5ft 7in would always say to her, with mock exasperation, 'Five foot seven *and a half!*' There have not been many goalkeepers of 5ft

7.5in before or since and there was general amazement that he was a goalkeeper at all and, what's more, that he turned out to be one of the very best in the Football League.

Gary Peters played in front of Death at right-back for four years, and when we discussed his goalkeeper's lack of height, he had a different perspective to everyone else I spoke to. Peters feels that it was Death's stature that made him the unique player he was, because he had to do things differently from a more traditionally built goalkeeper.

'Was his height ever an issue?' says Peters. 'No. He was so springy and because he was small you would just see him fly up to the top corner and get everything. He had something special that dealt with the height. He might have had to be so springy because of his height and threw himself around in goal so much because he had to. You would never see a goalkeeper as athletic as him, and I think he became such a good goalkeeper because of his limitations in height, which meant he had to be so much better than everyone else. A 6ft 4in fella might have just saved it, but he had to leap. For comparison, Joe Hart who I played with at Shrewsbury before he went on to play for England, was nowhere near as springy. Steve was so special *because* of his lack of height. He played the way he did not in spite of his height and stature but because of it. He filled it in with super saves and it wasn't just now and then – it was every single game. The way he played the game – that's why he was like that. I've never seen a keeper like him – he played that way because he was under pressure to do so.'

The fourth reason why Death became such a revered figure was his longevity. He played 537 times for Reading over 13 years, a record bettered only by Martin Hicks, who played for the club over 600 times. To play so many games for one club is a remarkable achievement, and his place in the folklore of Reading FC is secure as a result. It also speaks volumes for his consistency over such a long period of time. Peters said, 'For a goalkeeper to be that size, his ability to throw himself about was something else. His mental strength meant he could cope with anything. You could sign another keeper but he would only ever be a stand-in and he just wouldn't get a game. Charlie had so much respect for him, and Maurice did when he came in as coach. So he would have been in the side for ever.'

The best goalkeeper in the Football League

The achievement that cemented Death's reputation was achieved as part of the 1978/79 Fourth Division championship team, built on his extraordinary feat of breaking the Football League record for the most consecutive minutes without conceding a goal. Spanning 12 games and 1,074 minutes in total, which was extended to 1,103 in the first match of the following season, this is a record which still stands outside the Premier League.

In fact, Death's record stood for 30 years as the longest spell without conceding a goal in English professional football. His proud daughter would wait anxiously for news of a goal if any other goalkeeper looked like beating it, as would other Reading fans of a certain vintage, including me, breathing a sigh of relief whenever the interloper was finally beaten.

Death's figure was eventually broken by Dutch international Edwin van der Sar, playing for Manchester United in the Premier League in 2009. In turn, Van der Sar's record has stood for 15 years at the time of writing. Paul Bennett, Reading's centre-half throughout that record-breaking run, still says that Sir Alex Ferguson claimed the record for United on a technicality, as they did concede during that run, but Fergie argued that it didn't count as it was in the FA Cup.

It can be argued that either one is the greater achievement. Death's was in the Fourth Division where consistent excellence of this kind is hard to produce and the game is more physical and less refined. On the other hand, the strikers faced in the lower tier may not be of the very highest level. Van der Sar's was in the Premier League, where the quality of defenders and opposing strikers is among the best in the world. Set against that is the resources at the disposal of elite players, with specialists for everything from diet to conditioning to video analysis.

As Harry Redknapp told me, 'We didn't even have a goalkeeping coach at West Ham in the 60s; now they have coaches for everything.' He added, in a tone of mock disbelief, 'Nowadays they even have throw-in coaches, for goodness' sake!'

At Reading in the 1970s it was a similar story, with training taking place at a variety of local parks and sports grounds, and distance work being done on the streets of nearby Caversham or Burghfield Common.

One thing is indisputable in judging the records of both men, however. The kind of consistency and excellence to perform perfectly for such a long time is vanishingly rare; so rare that it has been achieved only twice in almost half a century. In fact, when Death set his record it was recognised with a Post Office official first day cover stamp released ahead of the first game of the 1979/80 season against Brentford.

As well as a personal triumph for Death, albeit one that he treated in his understated way with quiet satisfaction, as a job well done, it was an accolade for the defence and indeed the entire team. The 1978/79 season represents a Holy Grail for any team – a dominant campaign ending in the ultimate prize.

This chapter is the story of that season, that defence and that great achievement for Steve Death and for Reading.

Champions

When careers are over, times like this are golden. Reading were perennial under-achievers with just the 1975/76 promotion season as the sole honour in more than 50 years, and even that brief candle was blown out the following season by wage disputes and instant relegation. With Maurice Evans in his second full season as manager, having achieved eighth place in the Fourth Division in his first, there was little reason to predict what was coming.

The season ended with Reading four points clear at the top of the table, having lost only once at home all the way through; they scored 76 times and conceded 35 with just eight of those coming at Elm Park. The campaign finished with that famous run of 11 games unbeaten with no goals conceded at all.

Lawrie Sanchez was just 18 and still at school when he signed for the club and this was his first full season as a professional. 'I thought that was what football was like,' he says now. 'You turn up and win a trophy every year. It was only after a few more years I realised it isn't like that.'

Martin Hicks was also a young player in his first full season and talks about his experiences with a sense of wonder and excitement that he still feels to this day: 'That record-breaking season was the tail end of Deathy's time at Reading and my first full season. You get on a run and you don't concede and then you start talking about not conceding. It was unbelievable for me because I was a kid when I went to Reading. Every game I played I was astounded that I got picked. It was a fairy tale come true for me. Is this really happening? I don't think at that age you take in what you're in the middle of, you just want to play well. You don't realise what you've achieved until many years later. I was presented with a piece of crystal for playing 100 games, but I didn't think about it until someone told me. I was just so glad to be pulled along with the rest of them, to be honest.'

Maurice Evans was the man who put this team together. Hicks told me, 'Maurice was a lot better than people give him credit for. He was clever. We had some experienced players and some young players. He was very shrewd. I don't know how he used to pick players, or what he saw, but if you look back on his career, he would bring in players from nowhere, such as [later] Trevor Senior and Kerry Dixon from non-league sides; players who went on to do great things.'

Evans was steeped in Reading as a former player, first-team coach and now manager. Paul Bennett was part of that cast-iron defence and says of the manager, 'He was a lot more involved in the coaching side of things than Charlie [Hurley], and very different in the way he approached things. He would give you praise if you did well and would let you know if you didn't, which was fair enough. I thought he was a good man.' Steve Hetzke describes Evans' style as signing some very good players and trusting them to get on with their job and do the right things: 'I would describe it as a "manly environment" – you were told if you were in the wrong, but he treated you correctly and you just bought into the characters he introduced into the team and supported them.' Stewart Henderson, an experienced player invited by Evans to become first-team coach, says, 'Maurice was a great guy to work for – very straight. He was a good mentor to me on leadership.'

Evans was quietly spoken, but players knew that behind his calm exterior he had plenty of steel and was as prepared to let people go as he was to make unexpected and perceptive signings. Two examples show this focus on doing what he knew was the right thing for his club.

The first of these involved Robin Friday, who had so briefly shone so brightly for Reading that he was burned into the collective retina of the club's supporters. Although he had moved to Cardiff City and then drifted away from professional football, fans still hankered after their old hero. *Evening Post* reporter Pat Forrest ran a pre-season interview with Evans in which the manager hit back at the 'Bring Back Robin Friday' brigade, saying, 'If he was 100 per cent fit, I would have him back tomorrow. The fact is he is nowhere near physically fit and from what I have been told his attitude has not changed since he left us. He let Cardiff down twice and that was enough for them, and since joining [non-league] Hillingdon he has turned up for training twice. I worked with him when he was at Reading, and I have always admired his ability. On the other hand there are other influences which cannot be tolerated.'

There was no room for doubt there about what Evans thought. Neither was there after an easy 2-0 home win against a poor Rochdale side in the first home game of the new season. 'I was far from happy with our performance,' he told the *Evening Post*. 'We were very sloppy, especially in the last 20 minutes, and if Rochdale had scored we might have struggled. The sign of a good side – and I think we can become one – is to have no mercy. We should have trampled all over Rochdale and been like Watford were last season.' Evans wanted commitment, discipline and ruthlessness even in a relatively easy game, knowing that the team had the potential to be what he described as a 'good' side.

Success was built on a striving for perfection, or at least having the ambition for the team and the individuals in it to achieve the highest standard they were capable of. No one could have predicted how close to perfection the team would get come the end of the season.

Central to their achievement was what Martin Hicks described as 'a little team of five with an exceptional goalkeeper behind us'. Hicks lists the players involved and how they worked so well together, 'Paul Bennett was older than me and had come from Southampton. He looked after me and I did whatever he said. Chalky [left-back Mark White] was the most gifted left-footed player I've ever played with. Gary Peters at right-back was a very good player but had to work hard at it. Hetzke played in defence and later in attack and did very well there. He was going to win and if he had to take three players down with him he would take three players down with him. Great times.'

Bennett agrees, 'I played as a sweeper and Martin was very good in front of me. Steve Death was in goal and he wasn't letting goals in so that gave us a great deal of confidence. We knew we weren't going to let a goal in so we knew we could build from there. Steve was a big part of that.'

Steve Hetzke talks about the mentality of the team growing and growing throughout the season. 'We played some good stuff; it wasn't like we were just holding on in games. We had a small squad and not many injuries, so the same players played more often than not and you just did what you did. We formed a good bond and people didn't want to change things because we had success. You didn't want to get beat and you kept doing the same things, and we got to the point when we didn't want to concede. Even in training we were that bit more professional. You can coach with a smile on your face and play with a smile on your face. It's what I call "serious fun" and I took that into my own coaching career. You can tell the difference between a positive or a negative team in the atmosphere in training. It was a genuine team, there was always someone there to help you if you needed it. They were special times.'

Reading started the season with five wins in five games and made it six with a League Cup victory over First Division Wolverhampton Wanderers at Elm Park on 30 August. The match report began with the all-important word for sport and for life itself, 'Confidence. That was the deciding factor in

Reading's marvellous victory ... Oozing with confidence after five successive wins, Fourth Division Reading comfortably brushed aside Wolves to extend their 100 per cent record to six matches.' Maurice Evans called it 'the best result I've ever had as a player, coach or manager', before adding, typically for this football gentleman, 'I felt sorry for Sammy Chung, the Wolves boss and a good friend of mine.'

A match report singles out two players who had outstanding matches: Steve Death and Martin Hicks, 'Death, as safe as ever, pulled off a crucial save minutes after Reading had taken a 51st-minute lead. From close range, Derek Parkin hammered a fierce shot from ten yards towards goal, but Death leapt across and palmed the ball down before he saved the loose ball as Rafferty raced in. It was a brilliant save and one that certainly won the match for Reading. Big Hicks, who looks certain to become the bargain buy for a good many seasons – he cost only £3,000 from Charlton – was in brilliant form, both in defence and when he joined the attack.'

Death and Hicks continued to be pivotal throughout the season, and Hicks – then in his first year as a senior professional – would eventually overtake the long-serving goalkeeper to hold the club's appearance record with 603 first-team games, ahead of Death's 537.

The team sheet that August evening was to remain virtually unchanged throughout a season in which only 15 players shared most of the matches. That line-up was: Death,

Peters, Bennett, Hicks, White, Bowman, Lewis, Sanchez, Earles, Hetzke, Kearns.

Evans duly won the division's manager of the month award for August and Reading promptly came close to losing their unbeaten record away at Huddersfield three days later, falling behind to a first-half penalty conceded by Steve Death. 'I went for the ball and had it in my hands,' said Death. 'Gray carried on running and fell over. It wasn't a penalty.' As so often happens in football, however, it was Huddersfield's turn to feel aggrieved when the referee awarded them a free kick only to change his mind at the linesman's flag and give it to Reading instead. While the home players were still protesting, Bennett's quick thinking saw him play 18-year-old Lawrie Sanchez in for a 93rd-minute equaliser. Evans again reiterated his high standards for the team after the match, comparing Reading to the Wolves side Reading had just beaten, 'Thinking we were the better side and believing it would just happen.'

A half-time roasting from Evans saw Reading score three second-half goals and hit the top of the league with a 3-0 away win against Scunthorpe on 4 November. The match report from Graham Nickless of the *Reading Evening Post* again stressed the importance of Steve Death to the team, 'He was virtually a spectator for three-quarters of the match as his well-drilled defence coped admirably with what the home side threw at them. Then, after 80 minutes, Vince Grimes fired in a scorcher which most keepers would have been pleased to simply push clear – but not Death. He dived full length to catch the ball. A minute later the club's longest-serving player – he makes his 400th appearance on Saturday – flew through the air again to catch an in-swinging corner. It's goalkeeping like this which has kept Reading's goals against column to 13 this season and Steve must be the best keeper in the division.'

Martin Hicks played in front of Death at centre-half throughout that season and for several years to come. Hicks speaks glowingly of the impact that his goalkeeper's skill and consistency had on the defence, and on the team as a whole: 'There were times in a game as a defender when someone beat you or got to the edge of the box and shot, and you know when someone gets hold of the ball that it's going in. I would look around and think, "Oh my God, it's going in the top corner." Then out of nowhere you literally saw an arm or a hand coming across and flicking it over the bar. Your jaw would drop and you would think how the hell did he get to that? It wasn't just once, this happened on so many occasions. This is what made him special.'

Hicks gave me some of his thinking about what it is that makes a special player, or a special team, speaking about playing with genuine belief in your own ability, and not just knowing you could win but *expecting* to. In describing Death as a player and a person he told me, 'He had no ego. I'm not sure he even knew how good he was. The genuine people, the genuinely good ones, don't have egos. You have a hell of a job to get them to say anything about themselves. He believed in his ability but only he knew that.

'People used to ask me how I felt when I played. I can say that when I played against some great, great players who were a hundred times better than me [Hicks came up against the likes of Kevin Keegan, Mike Channon and Alan Ball] it wouldn't enter my head that I would get beaten. I thought that was how everyone else felt, and I think that was how Deathy felt, and he probably thought everyone else felt the same. He was confident but quietly kept it inside himself. He never said he had a good game, I never heard him come off the field and say, "I was brilliant today." He would save a penalty, flick things over the bar, but he never talked about it afterwards. He hardly ever had a bad game, but when he did, he would get annoyed with himself and then get over it.'

Gary Peters echoes much of what Hicks says about that season. Although still a young player at the time, Peters' first season with the club had been the promotion year of 1975/76. He agrees that the team and its achievements made 1978/79 special and gives his own thoughts on how it feels to play in such a successful team, 'As defenders you don't want to concede. Ever. So a goal going against you, even when you win, is not a good thing. I don't know how aware I was of the record at the time, you would just think you had done your job properly if you stopped the opposition scoring. My job was to make the tackle, get the ball and get rid of it. If someone got a cross in, I was really annoyed – it's a different mentality. In a later team I was in at Reading, when Trevor Senior scored, even when we lost, he would celebrate on the coach going home but a defender looks at things very differently. Steve was the same: he wouldn't think about anything but stopping someone scoring against him. You need the right person in the right place.'

Mike Kearney played in 33 of the games in that record-breaking season and puts the achievement in the context of the culture of football and the resources available to the club at the time: 'I played in that championship-winning side. I have a picture of that team and we look like a bunch of ragamuffins; we don't even have the trophy with us. I think a reporter from the local paper turned up and we just stood there and had the photo taken. If you look at Richie Bowman you can see the state his boots were in with a bulge at the side.

'Every time I walk into the Madejski Stadium I see the picture of Hicksy leading us off the pitch at the end of the Port Vale game. I don't remember there being a reception or anything – we'd done it and that was that. We didn't have our own training ground, we trained at Brock Barracks on Oxford Road, just walked back to Elm Park after training, or we would do some training at Prospect Park where the local Sunday League teams played.

'I look back on it with what I would describe as quiet pleasure. It was before Sky and all the money and publicity the game gets now but it was a hell of an achievement. We only had about 14 or 15 players who played most of those games, it wasn't a big squad. It was so basic, nothing fancy. You went in, you trained, you went home and that was that. Except for Deathy, who if he didn't fancy doing anything just wouldn't do it, but Maurice let him because he knew what he had.'

Mark White, who was ever-present at left-back throughout that season, looks back on that team with great affection. While he is alive to the danger of romanticising the past, he is equally aware of how special that season was, and of the bonds that were forged in the heat of battle: 'People always reminisce and think it was better in the past, but it wasn't. You remember travelling to these away games and winning and it was a great feeling. When I get together with Gary Peters, Steve Hetzke, Steve Wood and Sanch we seem to get better as players the more we reminisce and share our stories – we were all wonderful players. But when you look at these grainy films now it was so much slower than it is now.

'Within your team you've got your different little factions. I was young and single and hanging out with all the young and single guys, and Martin Hicks was married and would come in and then go off to his home life. Then you've got Deathy and Dave Moreline – I couldn't tell you now if Moreline was married or not because I didn't care! I was just playing with him in matches and then going out and having fun. On the pitch you're a team. When you're winning you're a tight-knit team and working for each other, and if you're losing that's when the manager pulls you together or you become individuals because you're not tight knit or close. The success we had in the 70s was because we were together and had each other's backs.

'The psychology of success is much more well known today than it was then, but you only get success when you're fighting for each other. Football was a hard game in the 70s, with tackles flying everywhere and you had to protect each other. I wasn't a dirty player, I never used to go over the top, but if you didn't get stuck in you would get other players not being happy with you. Good days. Happy days. I still keep in touch with a lot of them and I'm playing golf with one of them later today.

'When I leave the NHS, where I've worked for 25 years, there won't be anybody that I keep in touch with. I like and admire them but there won't be any I keep in touch with. Wayne Wanklyn, for example, I only played with for four years but I'm still close to him now. There's something about the competitive element of team sport that makes us lifelong friends, whereas there won't be anyone from my current job that I stay as close to when I leave.'

Reading's performances were gaining rave reviews from the most unexpected places, including referee Brian Daniels following the 0-0 home draw in a League Cup tie with First Division Southampton that earned a replay at The Dell.

Quoted in the *Evening Post*, Daniels enthused, 'What a smashing match. If only matches were always like this. I really enjoyed myself – it was a credit to football.'

The following home game, a league encounter against Huddersfield Town, was Death's 400th for the club. He was presented with a silver salver by chairman Frank Waller before kick-off, possibly the piece of silverware his daughter Alexandria knew was kept in the house but that she didn't know what it had been given to her dad for, 'He kept it and appreciated it, but it was never on display or anything like that; it was just there. I don't think that kind of thing was particularly important to him.'

Among a blizzard of statistics quoted in the press for this latest milestone were two that particularly caught the eye. Firstly, Death's record of penalty saves, which by then had reached 11 out of 39 faced – almost one in three and an astonishing performance. Not for him the premeditated dive to the left or right; he relied instead, as ever, on his reflexes, only moving once he could see where the kick was placed before flinging himself at the ball. Secondly, ten years after signing, the £20,000 fee paid for him in 1969 was still a club record, having stood all through the 1970s. The news was also announced that he would be offered a testimonial the following season. For a professional footballer at that time, this was an important honour, not least financially as there was the potential to earn several years' wages in one lump sum.

Reading lost the replay with Southampton 2-0, but Geoff Thompson's report in the *Reading Chronicle* again singled out Death and Hicks. Thompson lists two brilliant saves in the opening 13 minutes, firstly when he saved from England striker Tony Curran, racing off his line to throw himself at the ball and block the shot. Curran again suffered when Death denied a marvellous opportunity. 'Suddenly, as if from nowhere, there was Death spread-eagling himself to brilliantly block the shot once again. If Death was a hero,' he continues, 'then Martin Hicks was a colossus. His gigantic figure was prominent throughout the match, and he surprised many people with his speed and ability on the ground as well as his dominance of the aerial duels.'

While this was shaping up to be a very good season, a four-game winless run and going into Christmas in third place gave little indication on what was to come. The history-making sequence of clean sheets that made them into champions came in the most inauspicious circumstances, after a dismal 1-0 away defeat at Rochdale, who ended the season fifth from bottom. That defeat allowed rivals Grimsby to take over top spot from Reading. It also saw leading scorer Pat Earles twist his knee and the local press deliver a damning verdict on their prospects for the title – or even the top four – criticising their 'lack of ideas' in attack, their 'vulnerable' defence and questioning their character, stating, 'Evans must do something to lift his dejected troops for what will be a stiff test on Wednesday.'

That 'stiff test' was against new leaders Grimsby, and there was no shortage of advice for Maurice Evans to make drastic changes. The Rochdale defeat was on 24 March. Four days later, they thrashed Grimsby 4-0 with John Alexander, in for Earles, scoring all four. They didn't lose or concede again for the rest of the season.

After a 0-0 draw at home to Port Vale and a 2-0 win away at Crewe Alexandra, Reading returned to the top of the league with a 2-0 home win against Portsmouth. Goalless draws at Bournemouth and Hartlepool sandwiched a 4-0 home win against local rivals and promotion challengers Aldershot, and Reading were into their famous run. They finished the season with three straight 1-0 victories – the second of which, against Halifax Town at Elm Park, sealed promotion. The title was clinched in the final match, away at Port Vale. Hicks, Earles and Alexander scored in a 3-0 win.

History can be made in the strangest of places and the humblest of circumstances. Steve Death and Reading made their piece of football history in front of just 3,603 people at Vale Park in Stoke-on-Trent. The pitch was a classic of the time, with very little grass left on it at the end of a long season, and visitors to the office entrance at Reading's current stadium are still met with the iconic picture of Death, Hicks and Sanchez leaving a muddy Port Vale pitch.

The *Sports Post* ran the following article by club historian David Downs summing up Death's personal achievement:

'Reading's record-breaking goalkeeper was in action on 25 occasions at Port Vale. He had eight attempts at goal to save (three in the air and five on the ground), seven crosses to deal with, eight backpasses to collect and two through balls to intercept.

'As usual his performance was faultless, and his best saves came in the 38th minute when he parried a point-blank drive from Todd, and after 50 minutes, when he turned a shot from the same player round his right-hand post, after being originally committed to diving the other way.

'Port Vale coach and England's greatest ever goalkeeper, Gordon Banks, paid his own tribute to Death after the match. He said, "Obviously he has good players in front of him, but whenever we did get through, he did his stuff and made some great saves. He's brave and quick and has got great reactions."

'This season Death has added another PFA Fourth Division award and a Fourth Division championship medal to his already considerable collection of honours. He has now made 434 first-team appearances for Reading and kept a total of 162 clean sheets.

'At Port Vale Death equalled the Football League record established by Graeme Crawford of York City in 1973/74 when he completed 11 consecutive appearances without conceding a goal.

'However, in terms of minutes played Death now holds the league record. Crawford played for a total of 1,064 minutes without letting in a goal (11 matches plus 44 minutes in the previous match and 30 minutes in the subsequent one).

'Death has now kept goal for 1,074 minutes (11 matches plus 84 minutes at Rochdale) without being beaten. He can of course continue to add to that record in Reading's first league match of next season.

'Congratulations, Steve!'

Graham Nickless's match report for the *Evening Post* was simply headlined 'Champions' and was illustrated by a picture of full-back Gary Peters congratulating his goalkeeper with the inventive caption 'Little Stevie Wonder'. Reporting on Reading was not without its risks, however, as Nickless was to find when he was chucked in the bath by Hetzke and Peters, the pair having been given the nod by Maurice Evans. Nickless recalls, 'Obviously I went in the bath fully clothed and although I just about managed to remove my jacket in time the rest of my clothes got soaked through, so I had to drive home in an old tracksuit that coach Stewart Henderson sorted out for me, and wearing a pair of Hetzke's trainers. It was my one and only season reporting on Reading and what a wonderful time to do that job.'

Evans was delighted with the season's work and told Nickless, 'It's a great feeling. I had 15 years as a player and four as a manager, but nothing to compare with this year's experience. It's marvellous. We've certainly broken a few records this season and now that it is all over I can take the wife away for a holiday. She certainly deserves it, more than I do!'

Mr and Mrs Evans had plenty to reflect on during their holiday. Reading had just won their second promotion in three years and their first title in 53 years, Evans was named Fourth Division Manager of the Year and received a silver salver and a cheque for £500, his side had gained a club record number of points (65) in a season, and Steve Death had just become statistically the best goalkeeper in Football League history.

Playing with Death

Martin Hicks (1978-91)

Signed from the Charlton Athletic youth team by Maurice Evans for £3,000, Hicks can lay claim to being one of the best value signings ever made by a football club. Having started out as a novice professional at the age of 19, the centre-half played in every game of the 1979 Fourth Division championship team, and later became club captain. Most impressively, he is Reading's record appearance-maker with an astonishing 603 games in a 13-year career, overtaking Steve Death's 537 on the way. On leaving Reading, Hicks played a further 60 games for Birmingham City, becoming their player of the year in his first season. His experience has since been put to good use as a member of the Premier League's team supporting elite football academies.

The first time I went to Reading I was a very young lad of 18 or 19. I had no idea of what professional football entailed as I had only been in it for eight months in the reserves with Charlton Athletic. I had great expectations of how professional football was going to be. So as a shy 18-year-old who didn't want to say much to anybody, I walked into the changing room with all these expectations of how great life as a professional footballer was going to be, and there was Deathy. We were getting changed ready for the first training session and Deathy put on a red woolly jumper with a cigarette burn down the front of it. It was just the sort of thing you would wear in the garden. I looked at him and kept my opinions to myself as I was so young, and thought, 'Is this professional football?' He went out and trained in it – it wasn't cold, it wasn't winter, there was no reason, but he wore this woolly jumper.

When we went training he would take his cigarettes and lighter with him. He would literally carry them and pop them in the back of the net before we started training, and halfway through if it got a bit boring or he wasn't involved he would sneak off and light one up. It was mind-blowing at my age to think what have I come into, and surely this is not right!

I was very lucky to play at Reading for a long time and with an awful lot of goalkeepers, probably seven, eight or nine, but when you're talking of Steve Death you're talking about the highest quality and the best one I played with. Being a centre-half, you need to have a great rapport with your goalkeeper; you're backing him up, he's backing you up, telling you to leave it, get out of the way. Although he was a quiet guy, on the park he was unbelievable. I think he was the most natural goalkeeper I ever saw.

He was gifted. He was born to be a goalkeeper. Whether he knew that or not I don't know. For a goalkeeper being 5ft 7.5in is ridiculous. He was unique when you looked at him. Without any disrespect, he had longer arms than he had legs, I'm sure they were six inches longer than they should have been. They didn't stand out as odd but if you studied him you would think: your arms are definitely longer than they should be.

He never took training seriously. He didn't want to play in goal, he wanted to play on the outfield. He would play up front and enjoyed scoring goals. When he had to play in goal, and we had shooting practice he never used his hands. We were shooting from outside the box, 25 yards. He would put his arms by his side and save them with his elbows; he was so quick he could read where you were going to shoot, and for ten minutes he never used his hands; it was as if he didn't need his hands to be good. He really was extra special. Unbelievable.

He was different to everybody else. All the others I played with had to work at things, had to come back in the afternoon. It was different with Deathy, he used to walk in with his *Sporting Life* and sit in the corner, and say, 'Oh have we got a game now?' and go out and play. I played with him for a few years, and he was by far the best goalkeeper that I played in front of, and if he had been six feet tall he would have played for England. He was brilliant.

His height never made a difference. I think his arms made up for the lack of height. His speed of reaction was what made all the difference. Some people can work to become a footballer but the great, great players are born to be footballers; I think you are gifted your talent by somebody, same as an artist or a heart surgeon, the top-quality people are gifted with what they've got.

I don't think he took the running seriously because he didn't have to run as a goalkeeper. Goalkeepers now are as fit as outfield players. He would run around for a bit and then think, I've had enough of this and go off and do his own thing with the ball. Deathy just wandered in, put on his old red jumper and did his own thing. I never saw him in the gym doing anything. It was a mystery and a wonder that he was so brilliant.

Football was so different in those days. If you were happy then why would you move anywhere else? I think Maurice gave him free rein; he didn't force him to do anything. Maurice knew he had the best goalkeeper in the league and that you didn't need to do anything but make sure he turned up on a Saturday. He didn't say you have to do these press-ups or run this course. Deathy would just do what he wanted to do, but in a nice way. He didn't throw his dummy out of the pram and say I'm not doing something, he would just do it for five minutes and then slip off and have a drink. Maybe that was a good thing in his character, that he was so laid-back and perhaps he didn't want to progress any further, he was just happy doing what he was doing.

He was a quiet, thoughtful man; he was confident in his own ability and that shone through. He didn't have to say too much but when he did you listened.

Nothing bothered him, if we had a breakdown in the coach and were going to be late for a game he didn't get flustered, he was always the quiet, nice commanding goalkeeper behind everyone. It's only now when I look back on it I realise how special that was.

When you talk to old footballers I love the stories they can tell, they are gold dust and things that even their families may never have heard. They don't realise what they have to give.

I wouldn't say he was shy. He was quite happy to be out in public, to go to a posh dinner like the football writers' dinner. He was happy in his own skin. If you didn't talk to him he was quite happy, if you did talk to him he was quite happy. He would play cards at the back of the coach or he would sit with you and have a cup of tea.

Mark White (1977-88)

A one-club man who came from the Sheffield United youth system, White made 278 appearances for Reading in 11 years, earning a testimonial for his services to the club. A cultured left-back, affectionately known to all his colleagues as Chalky, White is rated by his captain Martin Hicks as 'the best left-footed player I ever played with'. White was ever-present in the 1979 Fourth Division championship team and an integral part of the defence that helped Steve Death to achieve his record of 1,103 minutes without conceding.

I scored an own goal against Steve from about 35 yards. It's etched in my memory forever. At the time I didn't think I'd done too bad because I volleyed it with my right foot back towards goal with the big centre-forward from Hartlepool bearing down on me. It went straight over Deathy's head and with one bounce went into the roof of the net. We just looked at each other after that. I was puzzled that he was on the edge of his box, and he was puzzled that I had knocked it back without looking. They always say as a keeper that you shouldn't be standing so far off your line, and as a defender that you shouldn't expose your goalkeeper by passing back from that range. I would say it was 50/50, that one.

The Hartlepool centre-forward had the temerity to run over to congratulate me for scoring and gave me a cuddle as if I was his team-mate. I also made their first goal for them, but apart from scoring one and making one for the wrong team I thought I had a good game! We lost 3-2 in the end. Maurice could easily have dropped me after that as a young player not long in the team, but Maurice was brilliant and kept me in. I loved Maurice.

Training with Deathy was a waste of time. I think he found training as a goalkeeper boring and would just knock balls away from standing without making any effort. It was a very Deathy thing to do. He was already doing it when I went there and no one had ever told him not to. Maurice was quite soft with him over that, and because he had never been pulled up about it he could get away with it. In fact, the whole team got away with stuff as well, going out perhaps more than we should do, but like Deathy we did the business on the pitch so Maurice was OK with that. We were successful because we were tight as a team and supported each other.

My image of Deathy was of him sitting in his corner seat in the dressing room, and David Moreline sitting next to him, both smoking. That was my image of him, cross-legged with a fag in his mouth. Then at the end of the game he would go home, and I wouldn't see him until the next match or training session.

Because of his height the saves that taller keepers would make easily would have to be spectacular ones for him. In those days it was always acknowledged that a goalkeeper would come off his line to narrow the angles, but Deathy didn't do that: he would stay on his line for the long shots because it gave him more time to skip across his line to the corner to reach the shot. I wasn't tall enough to necessarily protect him, but we had big centre-halves like Bennett, Hetzke and Hicks who would deal with the crosses. We coped with it naturally without making a big deal of it and collectively dealt with these crosses because he would be on his line ready to make the save. He did come for crosses of course, but you wouldn't expect him to clatter through the big forwards and knock them out of the way; if he did come he would always come when he knew he could take it cleanly, so it took that ambiguity out of it for us. It worked for him, because you're obviously writing a book about him so he was very successful.

We had a silly game we used to play up in the stands, on the tarmac on the South Bank. We put a chair at one end and a chair at the other end, and a goal would be scored if we hit the chair. I remember Jerry Williams standing guard of one of the chairs. Stevie used to get really involved in that. We also played head tennis over a plank of wood across the chairs, and Deathy and Maurice and all of us would join in those games – Deathy would spring to life, tackling and tearing about in the five-a-sides, heading balls in the head tennis games, but he lost interest when it came to playing in goal. Bit of a waste of time in training but a character and a great goalkeeper.

He was an enigma to me, because I was a young lad and he was older with a family. I would hang around with the other single lads and go for a drink and had very little to do with Deathy. He was close to Dave Moreline and spent a lot of time with him.

It's nice that you're writing this because those are the things we treasure about him, and that he was that height and could be a goalkeeper. If a goalkeeper was that height today it would be laughable. 5ft 7.5in and he could still do the business. You don't remember the conventional, you remember the unconventional. I would never call him Steve and I would never call him De'Ath! To us he was Deathy, and Deathy was a one-off.

6

Testimonial Season

Greenwood returns to celebrate his former charge

STEVE DEATH'S record lasted just 29 minutes into the new season, and it was the most supreme irony that the man to finally beat him was his own team-mate. As the match report put it, 'Steve Death must have forgotten what it was like to concede a goal until his own player Stewart Henderson jogged his memory with an own goal.' Henderson was player-coach and saw the ball bounce off his shin and into the net to end one of the greatest runs in goalkeeping history.

As it happened, the match report was wrong about Death's memory, as in those days before sport started taking head injuries seriously he was briefly knocked out in a collision early on that meant he played the entire match with concussion and couldn't remember a thing about it. Manager Maurice Evans wrote in his programme notes, 'When you think that Steve Death played the last hour of the game without knowing anything about it, it makes you realise it was a point won rather than lost. I shall never forget Deathy's save in the last five minutes; it's a pity he knew nothing about it, he would have enjoyed that one.' Nevertheless, those additional 29 minutes meant that the record now stood at 1,103 minutes.

Reading fared much better on their return to the Third Division than they had after their previous promotion, finishing seventh in the league but without seriously challenging for promotion, and this established a pattern of mid-table finishes that lasted for Death's remaining time with the club.

1979 also marked ten years since Death had signed from West Ham United and as was the custom in those days before footballers' wages ran into thousands of pounds per week, he was awarded a testimonial. This was a big deal for any player, with the chance to earn several times their annual salary from just one game and some associated fundraising events.

When he was awarded his testimonial the local journalist Colin Gunney was asked to join the committee and edited his matchday programme. Gunney was sports editor of the *Berkshire Mercury* and matchday reporter for the *Chronicle* and had known Death since 1972, when he took over from Roger Ware as editor and chief writer of the club programme. The programme Gunney produced for Death's big night remains one of the most informative publications of its type, with interviews with people from the player's past and contributions from Ron Greenwood, Peter Shilton and opposing players and managers.

Gunney says, 'We sponsored the Reading player of the year awards, and Steve won it four times. I presented the second award to him. He was a very quiet, unassuming person who shunned the limelight and didn't like doing interviews. If you spoke to him, he would be very polite, but you would probably get one-word answers. But he never refused to sign an autograph for young fans who asked him. He was one of the players who visited patients in hospital and spent time with the young people.

'Ron Greenwood brought a Young England side to Elm Park for Steve's testimonial. Greenwood had a lot of time for Steve and knew his goalkeeping ability. He said it was only his lack of inches that prevented him from playing regularly in the top division and knocking on the door of the England squad. My job on the night was to go into the England dressing room to see if any of the players wanted expenses for travelling there; not one player asked me for anything – Greenwood had left instructions that if any player asked for money, we should let him know.'

The choice of a Young England team to provide the opposition at Death's testimonial was both a tribute and an irony. Ten years before, his first manager Ron Greenwood had sold him to a Third Division club because he felt Death's lack of inches prevented him from picking his young goalkeeper for the first team, and because of that he was never able to take the England place his performances at schoolboy level deserved. Death, who could have played for a Young England side then, was now playing in goal against a Young England side managed by his former boss – the current England manager.

David Downs gives an example of Death's character and principles in a story that appeared in a different form in the testimonial programme, 'I met Steve in the social club after a game. I was teaching at a school in Tilehurst and one of the dinner ladies had a young son who was seriously ill in Royal Berkshire Hospital. She wondered if it would be possible for this young lad's hero Steve Death to visit her son in hospital. I approached Deathy in the social club after a game, explained the situation and asked him if he would be prepared to go and see the boy. Steve was a quiet, reserved chap and was non-committal when I asked him, mumbled something and I gave him the information and went away thinking that at least I had done what I could.

'A couple of weeks later the boy's mother told me how pleased her son was to have had a visit from Steve Death. Steve didn't own a car, and he had caught a bus to the hospital and sat by his bed and talked football with him for an hour or so. She told me, "My son has improved ever since." That was the kind of person Steve Death was, very reserved but there was a lot of inner goodness in him. He did it without any fanfare or publicity at all, simply because it was the right thing to do.'

Steve's testimonial dinner was held in the Co-op as the social club didn't have the space to hold the number of people who would be attending. Downs invited two of Death's former teachers for the game and celebrations, and they travelled from Suffolk and spoke at the dinner, and their recollections of his early years were a major part of Colin Gunney's matchday programme.

Also interviewed in the testimonial programme was then club captain Richie Bowman, a small, skilful and fiercely committed player who summed up the reaction of many people on first meeting Reading's great goalkeeper: 'Steve Death? Well, my first encounter with him was at King's Cross station when I joined the Reading team on their way to Grimsby for what was to be my debut for the club. Sitting opposite him on the train and playing cards with the other lads, I began to weigh up where everyone played. Steve I put down as a nippy winger or midfield player. It was only when we were in the dressing room before the match and he pulled on the green jersey that I realised he was our keeper! I must admit being a little apprehensive of him because he was only a few inches taller than me, but since that day I have become one of his greatest admirers. He's absolute magic and pulls off unbelievable saves game after game.'

His former manager Charlie Hurley, interviewed in the same programme, was also fulsome in his praise, saying, 'I have always regarded Steve Death as the Peter Shilton of the lower divisions. In fact, if he had been two inches taller I am sure he would have been with a top club. The three games I will always remember were against Sunderland away in the FA Cup, Everton away in the Football League Cup, and Wrexham at home in a Third Division league game. His reactions are brilliant and he is very brave and must go down as one of Reading's greatest ever players.'

More praise was heaped on him by none other than John Pratt, who was reserve goalkeeper, watching on for all those games while Death was setting records: 'I suppose I always looked at Steve as a rival, trying to spot weaknesses in his game which might have enabled me to be chosen in preference to him. However, he was always consistent and very rarely made mistakes. An instinctive kind of goalkeeper with all the right techniques, he has a tremendous amount of natural ability. He may be a bit on the short side, but his lack of height has never proved to be a disadvantage, simply because of his excellent sense of timing. Calm and unflappable, Steve never seems to get flustered, even when under heavy pressure. He is quick and brave also. What more could you ask for?'

Maurice Evans also wrote a piece for the programme, harking back to his time as coach at Shrewsbury: 'We played Reading in the Third Division and Harry Gregg [the former goalkeeper for the legendary Busby Babes and Munich hero], the Shrewsbury manager at the time, took one look at Death and said, "We must have a chance – there are very few good goalkeepers as small as him." After the match he had other ideas, and since then he has been one of his greatest admirers.'

Evans went on to reflect on his experience of working with him as Reading manager and commenting on both his character and his performance levels, 'Deathy is a quiet, unassuming lad who always wants to take the blame for everyone else. Always willing to admit his mistakes and often making excuses for other players' faults.

'As a goalkeeper I still think he is the best in the lower divisions. Brave, agile and quick. You have been fortunate to have a goalkeeper of his undoubted ability here at Reading. It has been a pleasure for me to watch him and work with him and I hope he has a bumper gate and many more happy years at Elm Park.'

It was typical of Death that he took all the testimonial preparations, all the tributes and all the related activities in his stride, seemingly unaffected by being at the epicentre of everything. As his daughter Alexandria says, 'Even when photographers came to the house to take pictures for the testimonial programme it still didn't feel like a massive thing. He said, "I've got a testimonial, and they want to take some pictures for the programme," like it was no big deal. I remember there was a photo in the programme and my sister wasn't in it, because she was about three and she kept crying and didn't want her photo taken, so he just said, "Leave her out of the picture, she doesn't want to do it." He was pleased that Ron Greenwood would be managing the Young England side in his testimonial, and he told me that Greenwood was quite a formidable character. My dad would have liked that, and I know he didn't suffer fools gladly.'

Roger Ware hosted the match at Elm Park, on 14 November 1979. 'As the teams came out, they let Deathy come out last. My line was, "And now let's welcome the star of the show – the star of so many shows at Elm Park – Stevie Death." I was delighted to do it,' he recalls.

Reading won the match 1-0, with a trademark early save at a centre-forward's feet from Death and a goal from young striker Jerry Williams. It was fitting that Death kept yet another clean sheet, but perhaps it was not such a good sign for the future of the England national team.

A crowd of over 7,000 turned out in what Evans described as terrible weather 'to give Steve the support he so richly deserved' and produced gate receipts of £10,000. The evening gave Death's public a chance to show their appreciation for their unique goalkeeper, reunited him with his first manager and pitched him against England's finest prospects, albeit in less than serious competition.

Real life intruded at the weekend, however, when Reading travelled to Chesterfield, went one up immediately and were then dismantled in an eventual 7-1 defeat. It wasn't simply a case of the Lord Mayor's Show being followed by the proverbial dustcart; it was a mess of epic proportions. Insult was added to injury when Death was booked for leaving his penalty area to prevent even more damage being done, and in an act of self-preservation the small knot of Reading fans resorted to ironic cheers with every goal conceded. I was one of that group and remember how our emotions turned from shock to disbelief and then to anger, progressing through acceptance before finally settling on a kind of perverse euphoria as the goals kept coming. It was our way of protecting ourselves, as the worst had happened and we had to pretend that a) it didn't matter, b) we could still enjoy ourselves anyway, and c) travelling to Chesterfield by coach to watch as the horror unfolded was still somehow a rational and sensible thing to be doing with our Saturday. A cartoon in the *Reading Chronicle* showed Death sitting in his goal with a stunned expression and surrounded by seven footballs.

A lifelong Reading fan who became sports editor of the *Chronicle*, Roger Ware says, 'Back in the day you could travel with the team, and there was a good social side to it. To go from being a fan to travelling with them was lovely. I remember seeing Stevie sleeping in the back of the bus on the way to the game – I think possibly he wasn't that well. They got hammered and the team gave him a ribbing on the way back for letting in seven goals.'

The mid-season hiccup threatened to turn into a mini collapse as Reading managed a 1-1 home draw before plunging into a 5-2 away drubbing at Blackpool and two consecutive 2-0 defeats. They recovered in spectacular style, however, with a 7-0 home win against Barnsley at the end of December to earn their first win in seven weeks, ultimately finishing their first season back in the Third Division in a respectable seventh place.

Days like Chesterfield, however, were rare for Death, and Ware remembers the impression the young stopper had made on him back in those early seasons: 'There were all these burly centre-forwards and centre-halves, and he would go up and mix with the best of them and usually come out with the ball or punch it away. He was so agile and so brave. He had a softly spoken Suffolk burr. He was no big-time Charlie even though he was the best goalkeeper in the division and recognised as such by everyone. He never had a bad word to say about anybody – he never had many words to say at all!'

Alexandria agrees with Ware's comments on Steve's bravery, 'My dad was pretty fearless. If he was going to get the ball, he would get that ball, no one was going to stop him. He had a really high pain threshold, and he had a scar because he had broken his cheekbone in a game, but played on because he didn't feel it. His knees were like nothing you've ever seen in your life because of all the operations he had on them over his career. He didn't wear goalkeeping gloves and even when he was gardening at home he wouldn't wear gloves as he didn't like to have anything on his hands.'

This bravery was perhaps most clearly illustrated by his reaction to having his jaw broken in three places against

Hartlepool in the 1975/76 promotion season. He played out the rest of that game and then travelled to Huddersfield the following week because understudy John Turner was unavailable. Charlie Hurley, tongue firmly in cheek, once said of Death that he was 'too stupid to be scared' and would go in at a forward's feet among the muck and bullets without a thought to the danger. Along with Jack Mansell and Maurice Evans, as long as they had a fit Steve Death to select, there was no way they would ever pick anyone else. Until the very end, that is.

Playing with Death

Mike Kearney (1978-83)

A combative and skilful striker and occasional centre-half, Kearney played 145 times for Reading in a spell punctuated by a brief return to his former club Chester City. Kearney scored 36 goals including ten from 31 starts as a centre-forward in the successful 1978/79 title-winning team. Kearney continues his association with the club to this day, having had a variety of jobs from running the Royals Rendezvous venue at the old Elm Park to supporting and mentoring the current youth squad, doing everything from taking injured players for hospital appointments to driving the team's minibus.

Deathy was a one-off. In my opinion he is still the best goalkeeper I've seen at Reading in all these years I've spent playing and working here. We've had some really good ones, a long list of good goalkeepers but he's still the best we've had. For his size and everything, he was awesome, he was such a natural, you couldn't have coached what he had. Of course, that's when he was interested in training or playing, if he wasn't it was difficult! I got on with him well, he was a great lad. I got him into golf for a while and he loved his greyhounds.

I used to play at the back sometimes as well as up front. Everything has changed with football apart from the ball being round. You see goalkeepers now playing miles out of the box. If Deathy shouted at you it was unusual. His natural instincts were phenomenal. He would just come out and deal with things. You would see the ball sailing over your head and think it was going in and Deathy would come from nowhere and deal with it. A cross would come in and he would deal with it, he didn't even shout 'Keeper's!' or anything. He was a different class to anyone else.

Dave Shipperley joined from Gillingham. He was a giant of a guy. Sometimes in games at half-time Deathy and Big Ship would sit in the bath together and have a fag. They would listen to Maurice's team talk from there; they could hear every word he said, but they just wanted their fag. Can you imagine that happening today?

We used to play at Henley golf course. Golf courses could be a little bit snooty and Deathy and I would turn up looking like a couple of tramps - I had threads coming out of my clothes and he had a jumper full of holes but they let us play.

Deathy was quite calm about games in the dressing room. He would never appear in a pre-match warm-up, some of us would and some wouldn't but there was not a chance of him doing that. He never wore gloves, and if he ever did they would be something like a pair of old gardening gloves without any padding. He was a great penalty saver. His reactions and reflexes were brilliant but there was never any strutting about from him saying how good he was. He was a diamond.

Steve Hetzke (1971-82)

Signed on schoolboy terms in 1971, centre-half and occasional striker Hetzke stayed with Reading for 11 years, making 261 first-team appearances and playing an important role in the promotion-winning seasons of 1975/76 and 1978/79. After leaving Reading he had plenty more football left in him and had a distinguished career with Blackpool (140 games), Sunderland, Chester City and Colchester United. In a long career, he made a total of 475 professional appearances before using his vast experience to good effect in a variety of coaching roles, including working for the Premier League advising academies for young players.

My first impressions of him were around his size. I was very big as a centre-half and we were pushed together into the same dressing room. He would only really talk to three or four of the players. Ray Flannigan was a big pal of his, they were smoking buddies and would go for a few drinks. As I got older I joined in a bit with all of that. There were certainly some interesting people around in that group, mainly from the town and not connected with football, and were into everything. The type of blokes who could get you anything you wanted because they knew everyone – an interesting crowd. They would talk to you normally, not as if you were anything special.

Steve was OK with them; he was different outside the football club. I think he got to know the people outside the club better than he did inside. The odd one or two used to go in the bookies, John Murray did and Robin Friday would go to the bookies with him, trying to supplement his wages. Did he need anything from the club? Probably not, I think he had what he needed with his family and the few friends he made outside the game. He just kept himself to himself a little bit more than most of us, but he knew his job really well.

We had a drink on a Thursday once after we won at Barnsley, and we were called into the manager's office. Alan Lewis didn't come in for training because he had fallen and smashed his face on the kerb. Maurice said he would have got rid of us but as we'd won the game he wouldn't. There were times when we would have what we called 'half a schooner of sherry' for lunch at the Boar's Head in town, but we did it at the right times. Deathy wasn't really into all of that.

He would smoke wherever he could and would try to smoke in most people's cars he went in, and of course in training he would always go out with his cigarettes tucked up in his shirt or in his tracksuit pockets, but the staff didn't take any more notice of it than the players – the comment was always, 'Well, that's Deathy,' or 'Mr De'Ath' as some people would call him, and there was total acceptance of that. Only very rarely would he come for crosses or throw himself around in training. He would just push them away or punch them, or let the ball hit his arms.

I remember him saying, 'Why would I want to jump for crosses when I've got you load of lumps there to head it for me – there's no need, I'll just come out when you miss it.' He was always there, always at training, but maybe not always for that long!

There were a couple of times when we may have had more than one or two pints of shandy. On one occasion we met up with some of Deathy's mates – all fanatical Reading supporters – and we ended up stripping down to our underpants and started playing football with them on Prospect Park, right next to the main Tilehurst Road.

There was the odd time he would come back from the bookies without a lot of money and would say he was going to ask the club for a bit of an advance, so he had some to take home to his wife.

When I played in my first game as a 16-year-old away at Darlington he was the one who was always talking to me, telling me to 'just do what you normally do, anything you're struggling with just let it run through'. He was the only one at the time who guided me through on the day and I had great respect for him for that. He was very kind to me on that first day. There's nothing bad to say about him, or his lovely family.

We used to make a pot of tea for the senior players and take it into their dressing room, and Deathy was always supportive of us young lads and was particularly good with the goalkeepers. He was probably more supportive of the young players than his fellow professionals. Mind you, I never saw him clean his boots though - we had to do that with these old wire brushes!

He was very gentle, it was very rare to see him get angry, although he may have shouted once or twice on the pitch but that was for football reasons. If he was a big fella he would probably not have been at Reading, but he would have been a gentle giant. His saves at times were outstanding, especially for the size of him.

He wouldn't have even got through to be a youth player at a club these days.

I was very lucky to be a football player and have the chance to do what I loved, and to play a lot of games. I loved it. I was signed as a schoolboy under Jack Mansell and as a professional under Charlie Hurley. I've got very fond memories of the club and didn't really see myself playing anywhere else. I used to talk to Gordon Neate, the groundsman, who had been a player in the 60s, and Deathy used to speak to him a lot as well. You could always find Deathy sitting in the stands talking to Fred (as we called him), another person who wasn't in the team! I was happy there until the club told me that they wanted me to stay but they were putting me on the transfer list, which didn't make sense, but I think it was their way of saying I wasn't going to get a pay rise. Chelsea had come in for me and wanted to pay £180,000 but the club turned it down. It didn't make any sense. I ended up leaving just before I had done ten years and left on a tribunal.

Stewart Henderson (1973-93)

Signed from Brighton by Charlie Hurley for the start of the 1973/74 season, Henderson had a long and varied career with Reading, playing 166 games for the club at right-back, left-back and centre-half before Maurice

Evans invited him to step into the role of first-team coach. He stayed at the club for the best part of 20 years and worked with every manager from Hurley and Evans to Ian Branfoot and Mark McGhee. He left Reading to rejoin Branfoot at Southampton; as youth-team manager he helped to develop the young Gareth Bale and Adam Lallana. He went on to scout across Europe for Fulham before moving on again to become a scout for Premier League Brighton & Hove Albion.

He was a natural. In the modern game kids are coached from the age of nine or ten, but I don't think Steve went through anything like that and I doubt if he had ever been coached in any specialist way as a goalkeeper. He was very agile. I remember in my first game – a 0-0 draw away at Newport County – we were defending a corner kick and the guy headed it; it flew past me and I turned around to see this figure appear in a blur and touch it away. That was Steve. He had this ability to get across his goal and catch shots you wouldn't expect him to.

In training it was difficult if you wanted to do something like shooting practice with Steve in goal because he didn't want to do it, but he would relish getting stuck into the eight-a-sides we did. On a Saturday he was brave and agile, and he would throw himself at the forward's feet and he would come out and catch crosses; he didn't wear gloves at all, and that's unheard of now. It's equally unheard of to think of a modern team having a goalkeeper of his stature.

He would say something if he needed to, but normally he would come in, do his training and go home. He could get nervous before games at times, but once he got on the pitch he was fine. I was like that, too.

Sometimes if the game on a Saturday hadn't gone very well for him, I would come in on a Monday and see him in the multigym, working out on the weights. He would be working himself hard; It was as if he was trying to get the weekend's performance out of his system so he could put it behind him. It didn't happen very often because he was so consistent and bad performances were extremely rare, but it did get to him if he hadn't done as well as he wanted. He was a great lad. I got on with him fine. He might not have enjoyed training as a goalkeeper, but he took the job itself very seriously. He really cared.

Becoming first-team coach was a great opportunity for me. Maurice knew I was doing my coaching qualifications and he asked me to help him out with it. I found it difficult to start with, as one day I was playing with the guys and then suddenly I was coaching them as part of the management set-up, so it was an adjustment for all of us. That Fourth Division championship-winning season was a wonderful experience though, we had a really successful group, and Steve was terrific.

My biggest regret was my own goal against Brentford. A cross hit my knee and trickled over the line, and I thought, 'No!' It happened so slowly but I couldn't do anything about it. Steve hadn't conceded for 12 games and had set a Football League record, and it was my own goal that ended it. The defence in the previous season, when we won the title and Steve set his record, was virtually unchanged throughout, but at the end of the season we lost Gary Peters and Paul Bennett who had both left the club. Hicksy also got injured early on, so I was only playing because Maurice asked me to come in as we had no one else! Then of course I go and score the own goal. I was talking to somebody the other day and they said, 'Didn't you score an own goal against Steve Death?' I only ever scored one own goal, but it seems to be my claim to fame.

7

The Beginning of the End

A less than fond farewell

GOODBYES ARE not always of the storybook variety. In fact, they rarely are. Steve Death's departure from Reading, and from football, was in keeping with his character, calling time on his career with no warning and leaving no time for anyone to say their goodbyes. Wilful, irrevocable, and definite. There was no announcement and, it seems, no plan.

After 13 years, Death was part of the fixtures and fittings. Gary Peters says, 'He was always there. You never had to check the team sheet; as long as he was fit he was in goal.' Until, one day, he wasn't. Team-mates came into work for the new season, and he was gone.

His daughter Alexandria remembers that it was a sudden decision. 'It clearly wasn't planned,' she says. 'Leaving Reading meant we had nowhere to live because our house was owned by the club and we had to move out. It sounds like my dad. He would never do anything that he didn't decide for himself.'

Steve Hetzke also remembers his confusion at his long-serving goalkeeper suddenly not being there, and no one knowing why: 'When he left it was literally a case of us saying, "Where's he gone? Has another club come in for him or what?" He didn't retire, he just packed up. Nobody came and let us know, he was just there one moment and not the next. Maybe he'd just had enough, and he wasn't in love with the game any more.'

Neil Webb shared in the general confusion, mixed with disbelief, 'Against Swindon at home, he refused to play. I walked in the dressing room and said, "Where's Deathy?" – he'd come into the ground, refused to play and buggered off again. I was 18 – I didn't say a word to anyone, I just thought: are you allowed to do that? I'd never seen anything like it.'

Stuart Beavon tells a similar story, 'All of a sudden that was it, he didn't turn up for training, and someone said he was packing it in and wasn't coming back. I think he made a couple of mistakes in his last game and he couldn't accept it after how good he'd been all his career.'

Martin Hicks says now, 'Whatever happened it would always have been his decision. There was no way it would have been anyone else's. 100 per cent he would have made his own decision. It wouldn't surprise me if he had decided he wasn't as good as he used to be and to leave. His mentality would have been you don't tell me, I'll tell you. He could be stubborn and dig his heels in if he felt he was treated wrongly. He slipped away quietly.'

What is clear is that the relationship between club and player irretrievably broke down over several months towards the end of the 1981/82 season, which became the end of his time as a player. Reading were in financial trouble and attendances were plummeting as they played out a season that would end in mid-table mediocrity. Interest and excitement were in such short supply at the time that after one home game, Maurice Evans found himself waiting in the press room on his own, eventually poking his head round the door to plaintively ask the stragglers, 'Will someone please come in and talk to me?'

The board considered an increasingly desperate number of different ways in which they felt the situation could best be resolved, some displaying common sense and some more outlandish. These included making the players part-time, putting the whole club up for sale and, crucially for Steve Death, selling the house he had lived in with his family for the past nine years for a price of £40,000.

The *Evening Post* took the unusual step of devoting an opinion column to the plight of the club, and the board's plans, applauding the suggestion that in order to protect Elm Park as Reading's home, players should go part-time and have other jobs besides football. The *Post* opined, 'Football is no longer the Saturday afternoon diversion for men whose wives go shopping while they go to "the match". The car and television have conspired against it. The old days, in that sense, are not coming back. At the same time costs have soared to the point where few clubs can balance their budgets. The only way out is to cut costs.' The paper then referred directly to the plight of Steve Death, 'After 13 years' magnificent service to Reading, now unable to continue, he faces the end of a brilliant career with no trade to turn to. It shouldn't be possible for it to happen to such a footballer – but it too often has.'

There was the usual claim and counter-claim, with Death feeling harshly treated and undervalued, and the club claiming to have offered him suitable alternative accommodation. One *Post* article revealed that the club were preparing to take the matter to court and evict their longest-serving player. Club secretary and former manager Roy Bentley said, 'It's a terrible shame to have to do it to any player, especially one with his years of service, yet he has left us with no option. None of us wanted it to end like this but what else could we do?' Death, who had clearly fallen out of love with Reading, and with the game itself, said, 'If it happens, it happens. It's the directors who run the club and they make the decisions. That's what it all boils down to. I'll take it as it comes, I'm not particularly worried about staying here now.'

Whether Death meant he wasn't worried about staying in the house, or at the club, or in the game itself was open to interpretation, but this was just the latest in a series of moves that led to bad feeling on both sides. Death had been replaced in the first team by reserve keeper Ron Fearon, and walked out on the club in February 1982, saying he felt unable to play football again. Reading then suspended him fortnightly without pay. When the end-of-season retained list was published, Death's name was not on it. It was difficult to say who had made that decision – everyone or no one.

Death's last three games for Reading – the last three games of his career – came in February 1982. These were also his first appearances of the season, an unthinkable situation in any of his previous 12 years with the club. The first was a 4-0 home win against Millwall, in which he looked confident and as good as ever. The next was a shattering 6-1 defeat away at Huddersfield Town, and his final match was a 3-3 draw at home to Doncaster Rovers, played in front of a crowd the *Evening Post* described as 'a pathetic attendance of 2,361' – and a team performance that left Evans fuming and frustrated. It also had a profound effect on Death.

Evans was quoted in the *Evening Post* as saying that Death had approached him on the eve of the next match – a local derby against Swindon Town on 20 February, 'Steve came to me and said he didn't think he was capable of playing any more and wanted to finish with football. I told him I wouldn't accept that and asked him to go away and think about it before seeing me again. But he was then of the same opinion. He didn't think he could cope with football. When I asked him what he would do if another club came in for him, he said he could not play football.'

What the club announced to anyone who would listen was that Death had 'walked out' – a pejorative way of describing someone who had come to the realisation that this was the end of the line. 'When it came down to it,' said Evans, 'he almost wanted to run away.'

While Death was clearly no longer happy with the position he found himself in, to describe him as going through a mental breakdown as some reports did is a stretch. Chairman Frank Waller was quoted as saying, 'We feel he has not been well and have tried to protect him.' Quite how the club felt they were trying to protect him by suing him to get his family out of their house is unclear, but the inference was that the fault lay squarely with the player and not with the football club. With the departure of such a popular and legendary player, this interpretation would have had some benefit for the club, in taking some of the heat off them. Alexandria, who saw her dad every day at home while all this was going on, is clear that this wasn't the case. She feels he was clearly unhappy with the way things were for him at this stage, and that he must have reached the conclusion that he had to leave.

Evans' concern for his great goalkeeper was real. Both men were part of the time-honoured process in sport, and life, in which the old is replaced by the new. No decent person enjoys it, apart from the young pretender to the throne, but it is inevitable, and the manager is doing his job by recognising the moment and letting it happen. The player, however, is coming to terms with the end of one life and the beginning of another; in his case an unknown future that he has not planned for or fully accepted as real.

I met Maurice Evans once when he was manager at Oxford United, just after their League Cup-winning season of 1985/86. I had asked for half an hour of his time to help with a management assignment for a course I was taking. He generously gave me three hours. In that time, he told me of a star striker who had come into his office ranting and raving and demanding a transfer. Evans listened until the player had finished, and then told him, 'I want you to go home, look in the mirror, and come back to see me in the morning.' The following morning the player came in and apologised.

I share that anecdote because it fits with his reaction to Death's announcement that he couldn't play any more. He sent him away to think again. But this time, when his star goalkeeper had gone home and looked in the mirror he didn't apologise, and he didn't change his mind. As Bobby Williams said in a different context, 'That was Deathy.' He had looked in the mirror and seen himself as he was: a footballer who could no longer play the game in a way he found acceptable.

The irresistible force – in this case, time – came up against a very movable object. Just as Evans was submitting to the inevitable, so was Death. Evans went with it, and so did Death: Evans patiently, logically and with appreciation of the difficulties for the player, Death with characteristic impatience.

Here again was the black and white, take it or leave it, don't hang around mentality he had shown many times before. Think of his refusal to put out his cigarette while carrying cones at a West Ham practice match; think turning down a trial with the Young England squad; think going back to bed when asked to play during a wage freeze. He was done and, as everyone knew, when Deathy was done, he was done, and he would have seen no point in paying lip service by drawing a salary he felt he could no longer earn.

Evans' reaction is entirely consistent with his approach to his players in other situations; Death's is consistent with his own typical behaviour in other past situations. Evans' response is human and very Maurice Evans. Death's response is human too, and very Steve Death.

A contemporary newspaper article, headlined 'End of the Death era', summed up the sadness and confusion at the way such a great career fizzled out, 'Quietly, almost unnoticed, the Steve Death era at Reading has ended.

'The long-serving goalkeeper, who made 537 appearances for Reading in 13 distinguished years, has left his club house in Tilehurst Road. He has apparently gone back to his native Suffolk with his family.

'Steve's departure brings to a halt eight months of bitterness between player and club, which began with his shock walk-out back in February. Then followed suspension, his eventual release from the playing staff, and finally the embarrassment of a court eviction order. Without dragging up the whole issue again, the affair is one which will undoubtedly haunt all concerned for some time to come. A bit more give and take on BOTH sides could have settled it in a far more amicable way, as Steve's service record undeniably merited.

'Hopefully, he will find peace of mind in the East Anglia countryside and maybe even consider making a return to soccer action. There are many non-league outfits crying out for a man with his ability and experience.

'In the meantime, Reading are now concluding negotiations to sell Steve's old house and another in the same road. They should realise between £60,000–£70,000 for both – enough to help ease the bank overdraft and strengthen the first-team squad. It remains to be seen which holds the greater priority at Elm Park. I know what the fans are saying.'

The now former goalkeeper's disconsolate comments included a firm decision that he would never play for Reading again, but they also clearly showed that there was no Plan B. He is quoted in different sources as saying he was finished with football, and others that he would like to play again somewhere else. It was sad that at the age of 32 it was generally accepted, by the press, by Maurice Evans and at times by the player himself, that this would most likely have to involve non-league football.

Death could have been speaking for many footballers of the time when he told the *Reading Chronicle*, 'I can't see me getting a job. I can't do a lot – I left school and came straight into football. I've no idea what I will do if we get evicted. There's nowhere else for us to go and I can't get a mortgage to buy somewhere if I haven't got a job.'

His career had effectively ended less than two years after the famous record-setting, title-clinching 3-0 win away at Port Vale that earned him footballing immortality: that was in May 1979, and the final game of the old 'invincible' Death was a 3-1 away defeat at Exeter City in April 1981. Injury against Exeter opened the door for his young understudy Ron Fearon. It would never properly open for Death again.

Death's game had always relied on his innate abilities – anticipation, bravery, reflexes, speed across the ground, and his natural 'spring' that allowed him to 'appear from nowhere' to reach high balls. As right-back Gary Peters mentioned in his analysis of Death's greatness, traditional 6ft 4in keepers could reach the ball with less need for these talents, while the 5ft 7.5in Death needed every one of them. There was also the cumulative effect of the constant cigarettes which, while fondly and humorously remembered by everyone who played with him or knew him, were perhaps just beginning to have an impact on his health and fitness. Therefore, while goalkeepers can play on well past the age of most outfield players, Death was perhaps finding it harder to maintain his incredibly high standards.

Lawrie Sanchez, a young player at the time, remembers that reserve goalkeepers never got a game when Death was there. Death's supremacy meant that he could get away with his habitual lack of interest in training because he could always produce the goods when it mattered. Suddenly there were these young lads, throwing themselves around in training and trying to impress. One of these was Ron Fearon, the man who ultimately replaced him full-time.

Everyone who watched or played with Death never saw his height as an issue, but maybe at the end it finally became one, placing on him the same limitations as on an ageing outfield player. This awareness, and the sight of the young guns throwing themselves around, may have made the training even more irksome, leading him to call time before time could beat him.

Death not only walked away from Reading, but from football. He never played professionally again and had no interest in working in the game in any other capacity. Roger Ware, who had known all the players in his time as a reporter and sports editor, continued watching the team after he stopped reporting on them. He says that Death 'was well liked by the team not only for his ability but for being one of the guys' but he saw for himself the former club hero's lack of interest in his old employer: 'I remember I arrived in my car for a match after Stevie had retired and he came past walking his dog. "Aren't you going to the game, Stevie?" I asked him.

"Nah," he said. "I don't fancy that." I think as far as he was concerned, he'd stopped playing and had left it all behind.'

The Death family initially moved back to Suffolk, and he attempted to pick up on his old life, living with his father and looking for his next option. As often happens, although back in familiar territory for him, the return of the native was not to be a permanent solution. They gave it a good try but he couldn't find a second career that suited him, and his partner and children were all from Reading. While Berkshire was hardly action-packed and its county town not a metropolis, the move back to rural life was quite a culture shock. Since leaving Suffolk as a teenager Death had spent five years in the East End of London and 13 in Reading, in both cases surrounded by houses and noise and activity.

Alexandria went to the local school and learned the hard way that life in a small country village was very different to the town life she had left behind: 'I would come home from school and tell dad about a boy I fancied, and he would say "yeah, you're related to him" so it was very different.' While it was her dad's ideal, Alexandria didn't like living there. 'Everybody knew everybody. If you went back there now you would find loads of people had never left. I'm not a country mouse, I'm a town mouse and it just wasn't me.'

'He enjoyed playing, but towards the end it seemed to get too much for him, and he quit. Knowing my dad as I did if he wasn't happy about something he wouldn't put up with

Steve Death shows off his England Schoolboys cap and blazer: 1965

BOLEYN GROUND, GREEN STREET, UPTON PARK, LONDON, E.13

READING Reserves
FOOTBALL COMBINATION
SATURDAY 12th OCTOBER 1968 at 3 p.m.

(H.T.-2-0)

WEST HAM UNITED Res. 7   READING Res. 1

1	Stephen Death	1*	Palmer
2	Paul Heffer /	2	Wallis
3	Bob Glozier	3	Biston
4	Eddie Bovington /	4	Tollervey
5	Stuart Morgan	5	Hitchcock 1 (PEN)
6	Keith Miller	6	Simmonds
7	Tim Clements	7	Henderson
8	Peter Bennett /	8	Brill
9	Trevor Hartley /	9	Bence
10	Roger Cross 2	10	Hopkins
11	David Llewelyn /	11	Maciak
12	Steven Knowles	12*	M. Palmer (45 MINS)

REFEREE: Mr. D. J. DARGAVELL (West Thurrock, Essex)
LINESMEN: Red Flag: Mr. M. R. HYNE (London, S.W.11)
Orange Flag: Mr. K. R. WARNER (Ipswich, Suffolk)

OFFICIAL PROGRAMME: TWOPENCE   No. 16

First contact: a West Ham reserve side containing Death, Morgan and Llewelyn 'hammers' Reading 7-1 in a 1968 Football Combination fixture

Outside the gates of West Ham's Boleyn Ground, with his great friend and team-mate Stuart Morgan.

A young Steve Death with the West Ham professional staff in the sixties, containing some famous faces. While the other goalkeepers in their traditional places are in the back row, Steve is in the front row – where he can be seen!

Steve receives one of his four Player of the Year awards at Reading from Reading Chronicle reporter Colin Gunney. Both men have seventies haircuts to be proud of!

PLAYER OF THE YEAR
COMPETITION 1969/70

VOTES CAST BY SUPPORTERS AT READING'S MATCH AGAINST MANSFIELD AT ELM PARK ON EASTER MONDAY HAVE DECIDED THAT READING'S PLAYER OF THE YEAR IS

STEVE DEATH

TOP TWELVE

1	Steve Death	1,102
2	Denis Allen	911
3	Tony Wagstaff	613
4	Les Chappell	412
5	Fred Sharpe	352
6	Dick Habbin	327
7	Gordon Cumming	102
8	Donnis M. Butler	87
9	Bobby Williams	79
10	Barrie Wagstaff	76
11	Terry Bell	61
12	Stuart Morgan	52
	TOTAL VOTES CAST	4,297

The trophy will be presented next Wednesday before the Testimonial Match against West Ham

THE COMPETITION WAS SPONSORED BY THE

Reading Chronicle

Player of the Year – and still on loan!

Watney Cup tie against the Manchester United of Best, Charlton and Law

BEST VERSUS THE BEST was the headline in the local paper for this iconic picture from the Watney Cup tie against Manchester United in August 1970. Steve challenges George Best, with Stuart Morgan in close attendance. Brian Kidd waits to pounce and Denis Law is in prime poaching position behind him

Death and Morgan in action against United's Brian Kidd

Manchester United's Denis Law hands the ball back

Reunited with Geoff Hurst for a pre-season friendly as part of the deal that brought Death to Reading

Catching a cross one-handed, while using the other to unceremoniously keep the opposing forward out of the way

A 12-year-old Neil Webb receives a medal from his idol Steve Death. Four years later they were in the same Reading team as Webb made his debut at the age of 16.

Dave Moreline and Steve Death at a charity event with actress Coral Atkins at the Merry Maidens pub in Shinfield.

Chairman Frank Waller presents Steve with a silver tray to mark his 400th appearance. While he appreciated the gesture, the tray found a new role as somewhere for his son Justin to store his marble collection

1,074 minutes. Reading leave a muddy Port Vale pitch after the game in which Steve Death became statistically the best goalkeeper in Football League history.

Steve Death's record of 12 games without conceding is honoured with a rare Post Office First Day Cover, signed by Death and the goalkeeper whose record he broke – Graeme Crawford

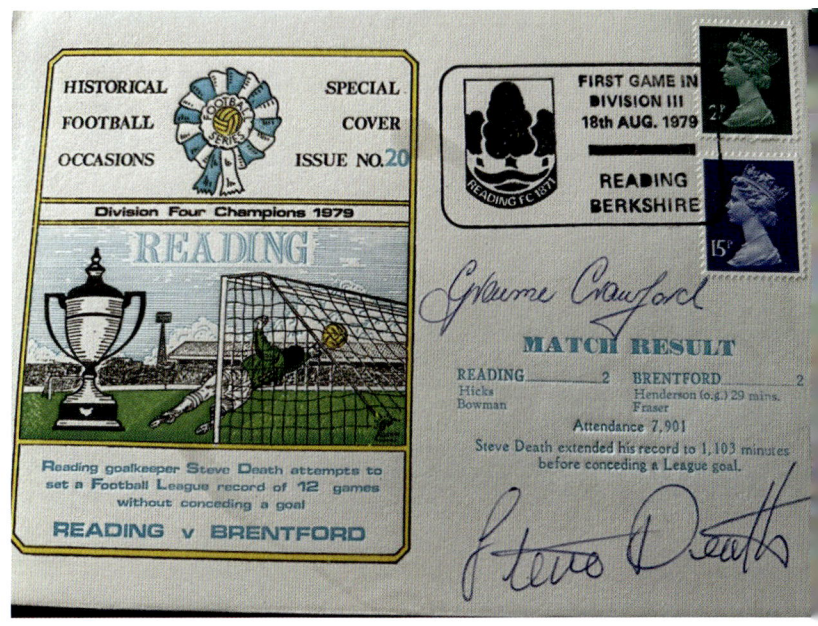

Steve Death: family man

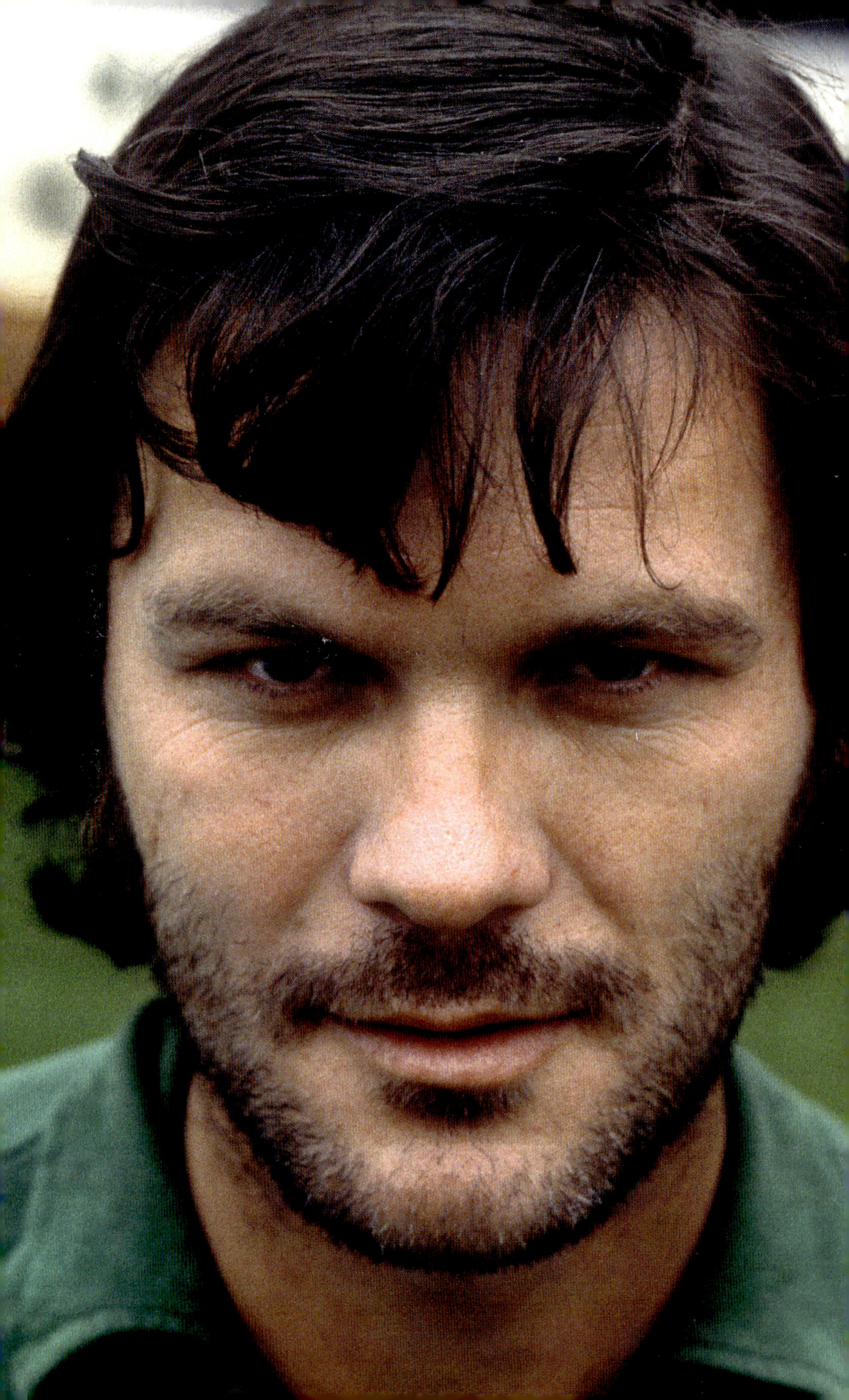

it, and he would just quit. When we went back to Suffolk he never played professionally again and just did some odd jobs. I would come home from school and find rabbits and pheasants and I would think, "Where did they come from?"

'People thought my dad was shy, but he wasn't really; he just didn't like attention too much. He would visit young fans in hospital, and he would give autographs, but he never spoke about football at home. I was nine when he finished playing and it wasn't until I came back from Suffolk at the age of 13 that I realised how big he was in Reading. When I told people my name was Alex Death, they would ask if I was related to Steve Death and when I said he's my dad they would go "wow, that's amazing" and I thought, why is it amazing?

'So I went home and asked him, "Were you quite a face in Reading back in the day?" and he said, "Well ... yes, I suppose." I had to go online and research a lot of it myself because he didn't talk about it. He did have a sense of humour about it all though; I remember they had a poll in the *Evening Post* about naming streets after the players and he laughed because his came up as Death Row.

'He was a fantastic artist, I remember he made a complete chess set out of clay, and I have a drawing he did of a greyhound – I nagged him for ages and then one day I came home, and he just said, "There's something on the kitchen table for you." Five years – it probably took him five minutes to do it! He also drew dogs, horses and birds. He could have made a living out of it, but he preferred to just do it for himself.'

Death may have left the countryside as a teenager, but the countryside never left him. Football had given him an escape from a life of sitting in classrooms doing what he was told, and from a working life of conforming to the expectations of others. Now it was over and he had to find another way of supporting his family without compromising his individuality.

Having tried going back to his roots, the Deaths returned to Reading, to live in Tilehurst just a couple of miles from an Elm Park ground he had no real connection with any more. His love of open spaces, wildlife and the natural world stayed with him as he negotiated a private life in a very public profession and when faced with the need to earn money to support his family after football, a job as greenkeeper at Mapledurham Golf Club was the perfect solution. Not only could he spend every day in the countryside, he could also work on his own, at his own pace and in the order and in the way he decided. He wanted nothing more from life than that and would undoubtedly have stayed there for much longer had his health allowed him to. Death was as satisfied with looking after his golf course as he had been protecting his goal at Reading.

Born and brought up in rural Suffolk, Death had reached this part of the Berkshire countryside by way of life as a professional footballer in London in the 'swinging 60s' and a

13-year career as one of the best-loved players in the county town that had become his home.

Bobby Williams saw the greenkeeper's job as the perfect fit for the now firmly ex-footballer, 'He was a country boy, Stevie, came from Suffolk. He loved nothing more than being out on the land, in the countryside, and he loved being greenkeeper. He used to have his lunch sitting under a tree on the ninth hole, he was as happy as Larry.'

Always the most guarded of men, he had never shown any interest in fame and all its trappings; no interviews with the press, no tales of drinking and womanising in local pubs. He met his future wife in a Reading nightclub, settled down and brought up his family in a club flat next to his workplace, did his job as goalkeeper and went home. Replacing goalkeeping with greenkeeping allowed him to continue as he had throughout his career.

By this point, Death was able to live anonymously, unmolested as he cycled from his home in Tilehurst through Caversham in the early hours of the morning – a grey-bearded working man balancing the tools of his new trade on the handlebars of his pushbike, of only passing interest to any stragglers or fellow workers who saw him cycle past.

His greenkeeper's hut was basic and functional, with one visitor describing a scruffy old sofa that looked as though the game was played on it rather than on the greens. Another, the club vice-captain Colin Gunney, didn't realise he worked there at all for a long time. Colin had been the *Evening Post*'s football writer for five years and had presented Steve with four player of the year trophies as well as heading up his testimonial committee at Reading, so he knew him reasonably well. When Colin walked over to the greenkeeper's hut to talk to Steve he got a polite reply, 'Hello, nice to see you again.' Steve said he had seen Colin playing at the course a few times. When asked why he hadn't come over for a chat, Steve replied, unassuming as ever, 'I didn't want to disturb you while you were playing with your friends.'

Steve was a popular figure among the other staff at the golf club, and subject to the usual workplace ribbing and nicknames. When it rained and he wanted to continue working on the grounds, he didn't put on a coat but instead made one out of a black bin-liner, earning him the nickname of 'John-Paul Goatee-beard', after the clothes designer who had famously introduced a bin-liner dress at the Paris fashion show.

Alexandria felt that the job at Mapledurham suited Steve down to the ground as he could be outside and do his own thing: 'People would recognise him and say hello to him, but he said to me, "How do they recognise me? I don't look anything like I used to when I was playing!"'

Except for his chat with Richard Wickson as described in the next chapter, when he was floating the idea of an ex-Reading players' association, Death was reluctant to engage with people on the very subject that had made him so well known. One man who approached him on the golf course to talk football got very short shrift. 'Are you Stevie Death?' he asked, to which Death replied, 'No I'm not.'

Playing with Death

Stuart Beavon (1980-90)

Signed by Maurice Evans from Tottenham Hotspur after Reading's 1978/79 title-winning season, Beavon had played under three different managers at Spurs: Bill Nicholson signed him as a schoolboy, Terry Neill as an apprentice and Keith Burkinshaw as a professional. He played three games in the First Division to rave reviews, but with the signings of Argentine World Cup winners Ossie Ardiles and Ricardo Villa, added to an already strong midfield including Glenn Hoddle, Neil McNab, John Pratt, Peter Taylor and Steve Perryman, he realised that he had little chance of a regular place. Beavon became a stalwart at Reading, scoring 44 goals in 396 appearances as a cultured and combative midfielder, including the penalty that put them 2-1 up in the Full Members' Cup Final against Luton in 1988.

When I joined from Tottenham and went to my first training session, I saw Deathy in goal knocking them away with his elbows and feet, and Maurice was stood behind him and he was diving all over the place making all the saves. The manager came in afterwards covered in mud and Deathy was clean because he was just kicking. He was something else, he was hilarious, but I thought, 'What have I done? What team have I joined?' It was so different to what I was used to at Spurs. And then someone passed me the ball and Dave Shipperley, who was massive, went straight through from behind and knocked me up in the air. That was one of my own team-mates, and I thought, 'Is this it?' I thought it was a pub team, honestly.

We would be on the track around the ground doing laps, and Deathy would turn up with his fags. Maurice would say to him, 'When you're ready, Deathy!' Deathy would say, 'Give me a couple of minutes, Maurice.' Then Maurice would say, 'Come on Deathy, just join in at the back,' and Deathy would put his fag out and off he'd go!

On a Friday before a game, Deathy and Big Ship would go night fishing and then turn up the next day to play. None of that stuff would be heard of now, tucking his fags in his socks on a cross-country run and walking, openly smoking in a training session with the manager aware of it all, lighting up at the back of the coach with the windows open to let the smoke out; no manager would put up with any of that in the modern game. But it didn't affect the rest of us, we just thought it was funny. I was a smoker myself, from the age of 13, and I used to drink ten cups of coffee a day. Ship used to live in the same flats as Deathy on Tilehurst Road, and if Maurice had seen the number of beer cans in their rubbish at the end of the week, he would have had a fit! It was a different world. Great times though.

Deathy was a hell of a nice fella, real character, though he had a bit of a temper – he used to play cards at the back of the coach and would get the hump if he lost his money. In five-a-sides in training if a decision went against him he would kick the ball out of the ground. He was very competitive, he hated losing, but on the pitch on a Saturday he was quiet as anything – he might say something quietly to you at half-time if he wanted you to do something, but he was always calm in a game.

But when you saw him in goal on a Saturday, he was just a different class and an unbelievable goalkeeper for his size. When I joined the club I heard all about this goalkeeper who had come from West Ham and broken the league record and when I saw him, only about an inch taller than me, I was quite shocked. But when I saw him play and I looked behind me, he filled the goal despite his size. He would come for crosses and catch them, he closed people down, he was fast, he was sharp. I never understood why no other clubs came in for him when he was so outstanding, and why he stayed at Reading so long – I guess it was just his size and managers couldn't get past that.

8

The Fans' Perspective

*Love letters from those who were
on the terraces*

WHILE TALKING with Bobby Williams over coffee in the foyer at the Madejski Stadium – the shiny new replacement for the old Elm Park ground, now renamed the Select Car Leasing Stadium – a man in his 70s came over to us. 'Excuse me, are you Bobby Williams?' he asked. After some reminiscence about games and players Bobby graciously agreed to a picture with the man, which I took. They shook hands and he left. Meeting his then 83-year-old hero had clearly made his day.

Tommy Youlden also told me about a very different experience at the Mad Stad when Manchester United came for a cup tie. On this occasion United left specific instructions that the players should be driven direct to the ground and be ushered inside, with no interaction with members of the public. Remembering the days of chatting with fans in the supporters' club bar after matches, Youlden felt the game had lost something important.

Neil Webb, who played at the highest level with Nottingham Forest, Manchester United and England, agrees with that sentiment, 'When I was at Old Trafford, we used to walk along Matt Busby Way before a game and it would take me 45 minutes to sign autographs and chat to supporters. Now at Premier League games players are corralled into areas well away from the fans; I was at a top-flight game recently and there were children standing by the touchline calling players by their first names and the players totally blanked them. It's a real shame.'

Steve Hetzke remembers the relationship with fans as good, 'People might approach for a signature, but most people didn't come over and bother you. We were very lucky compared to the modern era. One thing for certain, though – Deathy would never have been on social media if it had existed then.'

Mark White says how much the players appreciated the away support that followed them around the country, 'I would see these fans and recognise their faces when I arrived at these away games, and I couldn't believe that people would give up so much of their time and travel such distances to come and support us.'

There were drawbacks to the ability of players and fans to mix after games, however, as this anecdote from Dave Moreline illustrates: 'We used to pop into the sports and social club at the ground after a game and speak to supporters. It was a good buzz, but things didn't always go as well as you would like. Once, we'd had a bad game and I was with my first wife Pam. This chap sidled up to John Murray and was talking very loudly about how bad Dave Moreline was and making it very obvious so we would hear him. I heard a slap and turned around to see what had happened and Pam had slapped him! Albert Moss who ran the social club came over to see what was happening, and instantly barred the man. Robin [Friday] came over and was ready to help sort it out too and I told him it had all been dealt with and stood him down.

'On another occasion I went to a pub in town with Alan Taylor to talk football. We had an orange juice and talked about the pre-season as Alan had just joined from Chelsea. Someone phoned the club and accused us of being out drinking before a game and we got questioned by Charlie [Hurley].'

Moreline's experiences in the 1970s were of course well before Manchester United's visit to the new stadium in the 21st century, so the most damage a fan could do if they were so inclined was to make a smart comment or a phone call to the club; now players could be filmed and recorded. But Youlden's sense of loss of that easy association between the two essential protagonists of the game is still a real one.

As nebulous as the connection may be in all practical senses, the relationship between a player and a fan is as strong as it is intangible. Those concerned don't know each other and never will, yet they experience these shared moments with total strangers that live in the memories of both. In this book many of those memories have lasted for over 50 years.

The men I've met in writing this, all aged above 60, some in their 80s, were part of my childhood and adolescence. Their achievements were my achievements, even though I had no actual part in them. Or did I?

Gary Peters and I shared the memory of his goal from 35 yards in an away match at Brentford; at the other end of the shared experience scale, Stuart Morgan and I relived his own goal in the FA Cup against the mighty double-winning Arsenal; Bobby Williams and I remembered his first goal in the 8-0 win against Southport in the last game of the season; Mark White was astonished that I remembered a 35-yard own goal that sailed over Steve Death's head in a 3-2 home defeat against Hartlepool; Les Chappell and I both experienced his nine-minute hat-trick in a 6-3 win against Barnsley in 1970. I did nothing in any of these events, but I did share them, and so did a few thousand others. Our cheers, our delight and despair were as real as the players' and helped to define those moments.

As a Reading Sunday League Division Three (East) player I scored one or two 'special' goals and headed off the line in a 1-0 away win for my tiny secondary modern school team against a massive neighbouring grammar, but no one apart from me remembers these achievements: nobody was there.

Eamon Dunphy tells Roger Titford in *More Than a Job?* that he has no feelings for Reading, or for his other clubs, Millwall and Charlton. As Stuart Morgan told me, players often move clubs with no time to say goodbye. As supporters we only find out after they've gone and no one tells us why. But while they're with us – while they're 'ours' – their deeds are our deeds; they celebrate with us, and their emotions are ours. In a very real sense, our presence gives these moments their true meaning.

Steve Death, who lived a quiet life, never spoke about his performances, who went on strike over his wages, went home to his family after every heroic game he played, and who couldn't understand why people should be bothered about him, was also in this strange footballing alchemy 'ours'. As fans, we took pride in his deeds, and every crucial save was also made by us, or at the very least, was made on our behalf.

It is in this spirit that I want to give this chapter to the people to whom this quiet, tough, brilliant little man meant so much. This is what the Reading fans of the 1970s thought of their tiny keeper.

Terry Parmenter: I started watching my local team Reading FC in 1968, when I was ten years old. For me, two names always came up in conversations about Reading's greatest: Robin Friday and Steve Death.

Steve was better than anyone can imagine. I spoke to him only the once, and he seemed a quiet, humble and respectful individual. I was walking up to the ground for a midweek fixture, and there right beside me was Robin and Steve, both carrying their polished boots in hand. Robin just looked down at me with that smile and said 'all right' and Steve said 'enjoy the game'. I noticed Robin towered above me, but Steve was only a little taller than me.

People say he could have made it to the First Division if he had been taller than his 5ft 7.5in. His attributes were his razor-sharp reflexes, he was so quick off his line and fearless, he had this quiet confidence about him that commanded respect. For me he didn't have a weakness; even on crosses he was superb.

His unassuming manner made him the crowd's favourite and he set records that even today stand out. Player of the year four times and the 1,103-minute clean sheet record that was only just beaten a few seasons back.

Thank you, Steve, for wearing that iconic green jersey and giving everything for the badge. You were the BEST.

Clive Baskerville: I watched his debut against Brentford. He was the smallest player on the field and there was quite a contrast between him and the guy at the other end. When you looked at the goal there was quite a big gap between his head and the crossbar, but he was remarkably agile and had great anticipation. Once I got over the shock of his size and saw him making saves I relaxed a bit, especially as he kept going in at the feet of the opposition forwards and always coming out with the ball! I think that because he was a fixture for the best part of 13 years, we all took him for granted until he wasn't there any more.

Richard Wickson: I retired on medical grounds in 1996 and found myself with nothing to do. Our old friend, and former captain Phil Parkinson, suggested taking up golf as a good way to socialise and keep healthy. After taking lessons from the pro at Badgemore Golf Club in Henley, I joined the golf club at Mapledurham.

I was aware that Steve Death was a greenkeeper at Mapledurham, but I didn't believe I would ever get to meet him, although I would often see him driving the club's tractor up and down the fairways or riding his bicycle through town.

After organising several charity football matches, I decided to start up a former players' association at Reading and that I did in 1997. One of the first former players I decided to sign up was Deathy. I sought him out and asked to make an appointment to speak with him. One of his work colleagues said that he would not speak of his time as a footballer as that was in his past and 'only a job', and that he didn't think anybody would be interested, but I decided to go ahead and take the risk. How wrong that colleague was!

Steve and I sat down in the club's equipment shed on a battered old leather settee and, with a mug of tea in hand, we sat for hours speaking about his career at West Ham's

Boleyn Ground and at Elm Park. He spoke of the honour of being voted the club's player of the year by the supporters on four occasions, being given a testimonial in 1979 and of the promotions he won at Reading in 1976 and 1979; and of being given a PFA Divisional Award in 1974 and 1979 ... and was one of the first to sign up with the Reading FC Former Players' Association.

I wanted to bring him back to Reading as one of the ex-players we brought in to be presented to the crowd and do the half-time prize draw. It would have been wonderful for the crowd to welcome him back in that way, but sadly he became ill, and I never had the chance to do it.

Dave Goss: For such a small man in stature he was a tremendous goalkeeper. He was fearless and would always go down where it hurts at the forwards' feet and would come out with the ball every time. Steve had great anticipation and awareness and had a brilliant spring in his step when taking crosses, so his height was never a barrier to him defending his goal.

My most vivid memory was when Reading played Man United in the Watney Cup in 1970 on a blazing hot day, and he was outstanding. Had he been six feet tall no doubt he could have played in the top flight and very possibly for England.

David Downs: The other players had so much respect for Steve. He was totally fearless and very agile. He saved a lot of penalties. Whenever I met him he was very quiet but there was an inner goodness with the chap; there was a lot of depth there.

I used to do interviews with managers and players after games sometimes, and I remember interviewing Brian Godfrey, the manager of Newport County, after a game at Elm Park. I asked him his opinion of Steve's performance in the match, and he held up one hand and said, 'Five hundred games, and you could count the bad ones on the fingers of one hand.' This was a man who had been around the lower divisions for years and knew all about him.

He clearly set high standards for himself, because a schoolteacher friend of mine who taught Steve's son told me that he came into school one day, after an FA Cup defeat to Fulham, and told him, 'My dad says that if he can't play any better than that he's going to pack up!'

Another time, I remember interviewing Maurice Evans ahead of the last game of the season. There was nothing riding on it, as Reading were not in contention for promotion and in no danger of going down, so I asked him if he was thinking of giving a chance to any of the younger players. He said he might play Ron Fearon in goal, as the youngster had been very patient playing second fiddle to Steve Death all season. I pointed out to Maurice that Steve was about to set a record of 156 consecutive appearances for the club, and picking someone else would deny him his record. Maurice kept Deathy in the team. Mind you, I didn't tell Ron Fearon what I had said!

Deathy played more games for Reading than any other goalkeeper and is second only to Martin Hicks in terms of appearances for us. It was such a tragedy that he died at 54. He is never to be forgotten and his legacy lives on.

Roger Titford: Somehow right from the start Steve Death was endearing. In his first season, on loan, he won [the] player of the season [award] – in a side that scored 87 and conceded 77. The keeper should have been the least obvious choice, especially when he turned up ten minutes late for a vital top-of-the-table clash and we had a full-back standing in between the sticks.

There was something boyish, impish, about Steve, not just the small stature and shock of dark hair. He carried himself with a defiance, a belligerence you don't often see in goalkeepers. He was aggressively brilliant in goal, agile, brave and capable of outstanding saves. According to Maurice Evans he hated going in goal in training and he often didn't bother with gloves when playing.

The records speak for themselves – player of the season awards, appearances, the 1,103 minutes without conceding a league goal, twice ever present and letting in fewer than ten goals in a season at home. And he stuck with Reading for 13 years. It was an impoverished club and sometimes an unhappy club, but he seemed to find it home and I don't recall him ever being on the verge of leaving despite his wonderful reputation.

Ray Emmans: As well as being a Reading supporter since the 1960s, I was also a referee in the 70s and 80s and a linesman in professional football. I was at White Hart Lane one day for a match and met Ron Greenwood. He wound the car window down and we had a chat about football. Steve Death's name came up when I said to him that we had one of his ex-players at Reading. Greenwood said, 'Yes. Wonderful goalkeeper. So agile. If only he'd been a few inches taller he would have been an international goalkeeper.' So that was how well regarded he was by Greenwood, who was England manager at the time.

Whenever I saw Steve play I never felt his height was a problem; he could leap off the ground and catch crosses and he was a wonderful shot-stopper. I spoke to him a few times and he was a very unassuming man, very quiet and reserved. You wouldn't think he was such a great goalkeeper if you met him away from football.

Alan Porton: I used to see Steve in the afternoons and chat to him in Coral's on the Oxford Road. He loved a bet, just in a small way, nothing serious. At the time I was a steward on D stand, I didn't join the *Chronicle* until 1978. Trying to get anything out of him about football was extremely hard; chatting to him about greyhounds was easy. Studying form on the dogs was a hobby for him – a release from his day-to-day working life. I've met people from other walks of life, music for example, and sometimes they want to talk about something completely different to the thing that made them famous. He kept himself very much to himself, he was a really quiet chap – you had to speak to him rather than wait for him to speak to you.

He was the most unlikely keeper you would ever see, but he was brilliant and he was a lovely chap. He seldom made mistakes. He was one of the most genuine, straight goalkeepers, no fancy stuff, did his job and did it particularly well. He won four player of the year awards and when you think of some of the great players we've had, no one else has ever come near to that, so it certainly says a lot about him and his contribution to the club.

He's a person who is worthy of a book – if you ask anyone to come up with five players from Reading over the years, he would be in everyone's list. One of the most popular players to have ever played for Reading.

Pete Glanville: I played in local leagues as a goalkeeper myself and made my career as a goalkeeping coach, so I took a particular interest in Steve. I thought he was a great goalkeeper – after all, you don't play 537 games and not be good. He was particularly quick coming out of his goal and had quick reactions and was incredibly brave. He commanded his penalty area, and I could see from the terraces how much his defence respected him; when he came for the ball, they got out of his way. Steve was very able to look after himself and would throw himself at opposing forwards without fear.

It was a very different game when he was playing, and the role of a goalkeeper was different too – they are expected to be outfield players now, and to be about six feet four. Back then, it was a rougher, more straightforward game than it is now, more overtly physical. It was more honest but obviously not as technically good, and of course there was none of the scientific stuff around the game either. The characters have gone from the game to some extent, and there would be no room for someone like Steve Death in the modern game. It makes you wonder how many players the game is missing out on as a result.

He perfected the art of taking drop kicks on the half-volley, which meant that they were much harder for the opposing defenders to intercept as the ball left his foot with a flatter trajectory; this gave the forward a much better chance of shielding and controlling it ahead of the defender. The pitches were much worse than they are now, and when you look at that famous picture of [Martin] Hicks and Death coming off the pitch at Port Vale they are both covered in mud. That doesn't happen any more.

Alan Bunce: My overriding image of Steve Death is the mystery around him – not just how such a public talent could remain so private but how he was not pursued by bigger clubs.

I started watching Reading in 1969 at the age of seven so, for my first 13 years as a fan, Steve was pretty much a fixture. Any Reading team without him in goal was a worry.

My dad and I would normally stand at the Town End of Elm Park before it became designated the away end. When Reading defended that end Steve would trot down to the goal line and then leap up and grab the crossbar, leaving it bouncing up and down. I always wondered if that was to check its location, given his lack of height.

He was the only goalkeeper I ever saw who, when he took a drop kick, would let the ball bounce first. I tried to copy that technique when I played in goal at school. I didn't notice any advantage. I just did it because Steve Death did it.

While our best players would inevitably be pursued by other clubs it was a mystery to me why clubs didn't chase Steve Death. They must have just thought a goalkeeper of 5ft 7in can't be any good. Yet the evidence of their own eyes would tell them otherwise. As would his record of clean sheets and the fact he was player of the season so many times.

His sudden exit from the game in 1982 was quite a shock. I was so used to having the safest pair of hands in goal. How many more great performances did we miss out on?

In later years, I worked as a reporter at both the *Reading Chronicle* and the *Reading Post*, alongside journalists who would have had dealings with him. But none could tell me anything about him. I'm told he would offer a friendly nod when he saw reporters, but few would ever get quotes they could use.

One of my former colleagues tells me he visited him at his house to ask about his departure from the game, and although Steve came to the door and spoke, the reporter could get next to nothing in terms of quotes he could use. That element of mystery is probably what made him so interesting.

I later did some interviews with players of the 1970s but sadly we had lost Steve by then.

He died about six weeks after my dad died. I like to think that by now my dad, who was just as quiet as Steve, has exchanged some thoughts with him on the great times at Elm Park.

Adrian Porter: Steve has long been my Reading FC all-time hero. I remember him joining the club and the general opinion of fans at the time was, 'What are we doing, he's far too small to be any good!' Very quickly though Steve proved us wrong with his overall agility and amazing leap to reach high balls. I don't remember many specific matches apart from the one that ended his unbeaten run, ironic that it was an own goal!

He was incredibly brave in the days when big centre-forwards thought nothing of crashing into a goalkeeper in their quest to score. In between the posts for us on 471 occasions in the league, Steve is a true legend of the club and is held in high esteem by so many fans from the period and the years since. The Biscuitmen and the Royals have had many excellent goalkeepers over the years but none as committed to the cause as Steve. So very sad that he left us at an early age.

Russell Kempson: When I first saw him I thought, what's this diminutive little guy of five foot seven doing in goal, but then you grew to love him and you grew to realise how athletic he was. When he went for a cross he nearly always got it. I think we all took him for granted. You just knew Deathy's going to be in goal and he's going to be brilliant and reliable. He was this quiet, calming presence at the back. I don't think he said too much on the pitch, he just got on with his job.

I was a great Reading fan as a kid and I used to watch matches with my mates from behind the Tilehurst End goal. In one game in 1978 Mark White scored this amazing 40-yard own goal; Mark was one of the most cultured left-backs in the lower leagues but he just launched this backpass that went hurtling over Deathy's head and bounced high into the net. Deathy was standing on the edge of his area and had no chance. He just looked up, took a step towards the goal, stopped and shook his head and then went and got the ball out of the back of the net. Nowadays, a goalkeeper would shout and scream at his defender, but Deathy just looked nonplussed by it. That's how calm he was in goal. It made us all laugh the way he reacted to it.

I went on to work for the *Evening Post* for a couple of years towards the end of Deathy's career. At the time there was no PR or media department, and you got interviews by talking to the manager or meeting the players in the social club or running into them at the Spread Eagle on Norfolk Road.

I interviewed Steve Death in 1981. He famously didn't give interviews or talk to anyone but somehow, I got him to agree to see me. It turned out to be the longest interview I've ever done in my journalistic career!

It was just after midday when I arrived at his flat. I went into the sitting room and he was in there with the TV on, and it was the horse racing and he was studying the form in the newspaper. The room was full of smoke, as he was an inveterate chain smoker, and he had his dog with him. I introduced myself and got little more than a grunt from him, and I thought that I was in for the interview from hell.

When I saw that he was watching the racing I made a few comments about the horses and trainers, because I was into it a little myself and knew something about it. That seemed to settle Steve a little bit, and we had a few words about the racing. It seemed to build some trust with him, and he relaxed more and opened up a bit. We carried on watching the races, it was a five- or six-race card, and we spent the afternoon in front of the TV, with me asking him a few questions in the 15 or 20 minutes between races.

I was there for five and a half hours. I remember coming out feeling well chuffed, because it was so rare for anyone to get anything from Steve, and I would think it was the most he had ever opened up to anyone from the press in his life.

I came out of his flat excited but exhausted because it was Deathy and every little detail I got had to be teased out of him. While he was talking I would have to think, what will I ask him next – what angle can I go on now? I was knackered – I don't think I've ever felt like that after an interview; most interviews lasted an hour or so at the most. It was really good, really different, and when my editor asked me how it went I could honestly say I was delighted with what I'd got. He talked about Maurice Evans and some of the players; he didn't say anything controversial or particularly unusual, but it was nice to get a little bit of insight into such an enigmatic figure and to be allowed into his world for a few hours. It was a double-page spread in the *Sports Post* at the weekend.

Paul Tanner: Steve Death, what a keeper! Firstly, he has to be up there as one of the greatest goalkeepers to ever play for Reading Football Club.

If I was asked to sum up Steve in one word it would be fearless. Every match he played he would put his body on the line, in harm's way and regularly put his head where many players wouldn't even put their boots! Amazingly he hardly ever missed a game through injury!

TINY KEEPER

I'm sure many teams looked at his diminutive figure warming up in goal and thought they'd have a field day with high balls into the box and shots into the four corners of the goal. How wrong they frequently were when at the end of a game he'd more often than not won his team the game single-handedly with a man of the match performance. The fact that he was voted by the fans as the club's player of the season on four occasions, no player in the history of the club has won it more times, says it all really. He was loved and appreciated by every single fan.

Apart from his bravery he was a good shot-stopper, dominated his box, had a decent leap, was extremely agile and possessed a good kick. Another great quality was his safe pair of hands and unlike most other keepers he never wore gloves. He was a terrific last line of defence.

In the 1978/79 season plus one game in 1979/80 he set a record of 1,103 minutes without conceding a goal. The record only came to an end when one of his own defenders put the ball past him!

Many often said that if he'd been a few inches taller with his undoubted ability he'd have played for a top club and been an international goalkeeper. He was that good. If he was playing today he'd be worth a fortune!

Legend is generally an overused word in sport, but Steve Death deserves the accolade as he was and always will be a true legend for Reading Football Club.

Melanie Bishop: I wrote this poem in 2003 just after his death, without any real idea of what to do with it at the time. I just tried to document the impact he had for Reading Football Club. It has been saved in my documents until now – perhaps it was just waiting for someone to write a book about Steve Death.

The Keeper of the Net
Some men are born to create records
Some are destined to leave their mark
One man did just this, his stage
Our beloved Elm Park.

In stature he may have been small
But he was a Colossus between the sticks
He always gave his all
He denied many a magician and thwarted many a trick.

In height he was just five foot seven
But played as if he was seven foot five
There wasn't a part of that goalmouth
That Steve Death couldn't dive.

1,103 minutes the record books do say
Of an English record still unbroken
Steve Death had barred the way,
His name with reverence spoken,
He kept them all at bay.

TINY KEEPER

When his playing days were done
He hung up his football boots
No longer number one
He headed for his roots.

Reading fans will always remember,
Not one will ever forget
Our goalie Steve Death
The keeper of the net.

Playing with Death

Neil Webb (1979-82)

Joining his boyhood club straight from Little Heath School in Tilehurst, Webb's debut in 1980 as a 16-year-old made him Reading's youngest ever player. As the son of former Reading hero Douggie Webb, and with his mum working in the club's office, he came from a family of Reading 'royalty'. After scoring 22 goals from midfield in 72 appearances, he left for Portsmouth in 1980 for a tribunal-set fee of £87,500 and went on to have a stellar career, initially playing for Alan Ball at Pompey, then with Brian Clough's Nottingham Forest and Alex Ferguson's Manchester United. Webb played 26 times for England under Bobby Robson, scoring four international goals, and was part of the Italia 90 World Cup squad.

Playing for Reading was all I ever wanted to do. I used to stand outside the players' entrance with my autograph book – there were only about 16 players in the first-team squad, and I got the autographs of each player multiple times. They used to say to me, 'You've already got mine, what do you want it again for?'

I used to be at the ground all the time as a kid, with my dad working at the club as reserve-team manager and my mum being in the office. I was on the terraces every week, watching from behind the goal at the town end. I loved it there. I used to queue up for my half-time Bovril and packet of crisps in the little kiosk behind the goal. I remember the Arsenal game, sitting on the cinder track in front of D stand, watching Steve in goal against that great Arsenal team.

Steve was my idol. I have a photo of him presenting me with a medal when I was about 12 years old. It was the end of the season; I was playing for Southcote, and we had won the league and Steve came and presented the medals to us. I think he said 'congratulations' and that was it. He knew vaguely who I was because my dad was at the club, so he had seen me around. People told me that he wouldn't turn up because he didn't like having his picture taken and all that attention, so I couldn't believe that I had actually got to meet him. I'd been watching him from behind the goal and there I was, standing next to him; it was surreal.

Four years later I got to play with him in the first team – I was 16 years old. Looking at the photo now, he's wearing a suit and a tie that's done up very tight and very straight and I can see how uncomfortable he looks in it – he was never much of a formal dresser!

A lot of the time when we trained at Brock Barracks on the Oxford Road, we didn't have goals and played with jumpers for goalposts like kids playing in the park. Other times the apprentices would carry the five-a-side goals round. Depending on his mood, Deathy would either do his usual routine and take the mickey by saving shots with his elbows, feet or head, or he would dive all over the place to keep them out: either way, he used to make sure we didn't get past him.

Steve was great. He had his spot in the dressing room, walked in with his fags, did his training and then buggered off. He was great with me, always encouraging. Great leap, great shot-stopper.

He was very confident in his own ability, but without the arrogance. The arrogance was within, which is a great thing to have. If you're that good you don't need to shout about it; your fellow pros and supporters can see it for themselves. He had that inner confidence, but he never showed it – whether that was a good thing for him or not, to keep everything bottled up, I don't know. You would say he was the ultimate pro apart from all the smoking.

He wasn't a shouter in goal. Even at corners it would be one of the others who told me where to go and who to mark, it wasn't Deathy. He would come off his line for the ball and if he did that, Martin and the rest of the defence just knew he was going to catch it. As a shot-stopper he was the best in his time I reckon, and the best goalkeeper we ever had. We've had some characters here – he was the quietest of the lot, and probably the best of the lot.

My dream had always been to play for Reading, but when my first contract was up no one spoke to me about a new one, so when Portsmouth came in for me I went and spoke to them. When I got back to Reading, Maurice [Evans] asked me what I wanted to do. I said I didn't know. I didn't understand the business side of football, or that it wasn't always very nice. I just said to Maurice, 'I've signed for Portsmouth,' and he said, 'You can't do that!' It turned out that Reading had just accepted a bid from Chelsea for much more money, but nobody had told me and I had signed for Portsmouth thinking I was free to do so. I stepped aside at that point and let my dad talk to Maurice, because they had played together at Reading and knew each other well. The fee was eventually set by tribunal at £87,500 which was much less than Chelsea had offered for me, so Reading lost out on a lot of money. It all got a bit messy and my mum and dad both left the club as a result.

It was all done so differently then. I remember playing Chester away, and after the match we were on the team bus and Mike Kearney got on with his muddy boots. Mike had left us to go back to Chester a few months before and suddenly there he was – he'd been playing in the match for Chester and he got on our coach after the game and said, 'I've just signed for you again.'

9

The End, and Final Thoughts

Death, and some perspective

STEVE DEATH passed away on 26 October 2003 at the age of 54. He had suffered from cancer for some time, receiving treatment until it became clear that he would not recover, when he was moved to the Duchess of Kent Hospice in Liebenrood Road, next to Prospect Park where he had trained so often with the Reading first team. Prospect Park was just a few hundred yards away from the site of the old Elm Park, scene of so many memorable moments.

Martin Hicks was one of many who was affected and saddened by his team-mate's early passing, 'I was shocked by his death and went to his funeral. He kept his own countenance. He was quite a shy lad. Others were full of themselves and trying to prove themselves, but Deathy didn't have to prove himself. Good goalkeeper, quiet man, honest man. I can't remember going out for a drink with him – I was ten years younger so we wouldn't have been

THE END, AND FINAL THOUGHTS

socially friendly. We spent all that time together but I didn't really know him.'

Bobby Williams, who was Steve's captain in the early years at Reading, and who knew him very well, kept up his friendship with his younger team-mate until the very end: 'When he got cancer I used to go and see him and he was in bed with his oxygen, and when he moved to Battle Hospital I used to go and see him there, and then he went into the hospice and I used to go and see him in there. He was cheerful to the end. The last time I saw him I said I was going on holiday. Deathy said, you go and enjoy it, I'll see you when you get back. He'd passed on by the time I got back.'

When news broke of his death, there was an outpouring of grief in the town, and from those who had moved away but treasured their memories of his 13 years in Reading and the teams he'd played with in that time. Steve's funeral was front-page news in the local papers, with a host of former team-mates attending the town's crematorium to pay their respects. The *Evening Post* asked if the family would mind if they printed photographs of family members at the funeral, to which Alexandria said they most definitely would mind. The paper instead carried a picture of his hearse alongside the article. While this reflected her dad's importance to the people of the town, it was still an unwelcome intrusion, and she wondered why they couldn't have simply printed pictures of him from his playing days.

It was a simple, humanist ceremony, with his favourite music playing and Alexandria reading a poem she had written in tribute to him. One of the songs played was Nat King Cole's 'Unforgettable'. Colin Gunney, the *Reading Chronicle* reporter who had presented Steve with so many player of the year awards, gave one of the funeral orations; David Downs, the hugely respected club historian and keeper of all things Reading, gave the other. Gunney had known Steve professionally through his reporting duties, his contributions to Reading programmes, and as editor of the testimonial programme. He was also a club captain at Mapledurham Golf Club. Downs had made countless contributions to books, programmes and newspaper articles and conducted interviews with people involved in all aspects of the club. Both men were members of the testimonial committee, for which a grateful goalkeeper had presented them each with an inscribed whiskey decanter and glasses.

Among the mourners were Reading players past and present, and club officials – a roll call of the club's recent history featuring backroom staff, supporters and journalists, including Steve Hetzke, Lawrie Sanchez, Stewart Henderson, Tom Ryan, Jerry Williams, Stuart Beavon, Bobby Williams, Terry Bell, Mike Kearney, Johnny Walker, Kenny Price, Nicky Hammond, Charlie Hurley, Ron Grant and Gordon Neate.

Steve was true to himself until the end, spending what was left of his time on the planet being with his family, his few close friends and, for as long as he could, his greyhounds. Also, he spent time with a copy of the *Racing Post* and the inevitable 20 Embassy. Bobby Williams' phrase springs to mind again, 'That was Deathy.'

As fellow player Mark White said to me, 'You remember the unusual ones,' and Steve Death was unique. He was a man of contradictions, who did things his way and lived his life very much on his own terms. The goalkeeper who never played in goal in practice matches and refused to dive in training. The quiet man who was a local superstar. The man who was the 'wrong' size and build for his specialist role in the team but who became the very best at it. The professional athlete who smoked and ducked out of running and exercise but went on to create club and national records. The young player with the 'George Best looks' who preferred a quiet pint with his mates ahead of the 'swinging 60s' lifestyle in the East End of London.

It is also telling that while his team-mate Stuart Morgan still has the trophy for winning a youth competition in Switzerland in 1969 and keeps it in pride of place along with other mementos of his career, Steve allowed his commemorative plate for playing 400 matches for Reading to be used to store his son's collection of marbles.

His behaviour was not an affectation but simply an expression of who he was and what he saw as important. It wasn't done for any kind of pay-off or effect. He was a person who had strong likes and preferences and who lived by his own code. While he formed a few close friendships in football he showed little interest in the game outside his role in it; he was a loyal and principled man who looked after the well-being of those who were vulnerable. Paul Bennett, centre-half and captain of the 1979 championship team, says, 'He was an odd person in many ways. Very quiet. You really didn't get to know much about him at all. He just got on with things. He would come in at a time that suited him, get changed and train.' Wayne Wanklyn and Steve Hetzke, both teenagers and apprentices when they first played with Steve, remember his practical and unshowy kindness and consideration at times when they needed it.

As well as being such an individual, Steve was also part of the era he operated in, the social context and the state of the game in the 1960s and 70s. He played in an era in which footballers were heroes to many but were paid no better than the people who came to watch them, leaving him to bring up his family in a club house on a peppercorn rent which he had to vacate when he finished playing. Sports science hadn't been thought of in an era when, as his team-mate and friend Dave Moreline says, you would get up in the morning on a matchday and have a full English before travelling to the ground. Steve would sit and have a fag with Moreline or Tony Wagstaff in the dressing room before kick-off and listen to the manager's team talk while smoking.

There was more room for mavericks in an era in which George Best (who Robin Friday modelled himself on as a boy) and Frank Worthington graced the old First Division along with Rodney Marsh and Stan Bowles. In the Fourth Division, Charlie Hurley as Reading manager risked his own mavericks in Friday and John Murray – briefly a teenage goalscoring sensation for First Division Burnley who joined Reading after being sacked by Bury for fighting with his manager.

Football was also at times a brutal game in the 1970s, on the field and off it. On the park there was cynicism and niggling, and off the pitch there was violence, with the birth of hooliganism and some grounds that players and fans knew would be physically intimidating. It was not a job for the faint-hearted. Stuart Beavon, a ball-playing midfielder who joined the club as the decade ended, found himself on debut being wiped out from behind the first two times he received the ball; becoming aware that the referee didn't seem to notice, Beavon decided that he would have to leave his foot with studs up behind him to prevent it from happening again.

Many of the players from Steve's era are still in touch today and as close as ever. Mark White, left-back for Reading for many years, told me that when he retires from the NHS, for whom he has worked for 25 years, he knows he will not feel the bond with his former colleagues that he still shares with his old team-mates at Elm Park. He feels that the heightened experience and passion of competitive sport creates a sense of belonging and togetherness that he hasn't felt since, much as he likes and respects his current work-mates.

This is also true for supporters, in many ways even more so, as once we have committed ourselves to a team, we have little or no choice in the matter and are stuck with our allegiance for life. I remember hearing of one man who changed the team he supported to a more fashionable one. A mutual acquaintance simply shook his head and pronounced, 'You can never trust someone who changes the football team he supports.' Players can move on, but fans can't.

David Downs took his lifelong dedication to the extreme when he asked the club for permission to spend the last night at Elm Park before the demolition men moved in. He took his sleeping bag and slept all night in the centre circle. He recalls, 'My first game was in 1947 when I went with my dad. I didn't understand what was going on, but there were lots of people in coloured shirts running up and down, and I was leaning on the wall with my dad behind me, and five minutes in I was hooked.' He describes the experience of sitting in the centre circle decades later and looking around him at the deserted old ground: 'As I lay there, I could see all the old players – Johnny Walker, Ron Blackman, Jimmy Wheeler, all of them – as they were when I used to watch them; they were right there in front of me and as real to me then as they had been all those years ago.'

David is a self-confessed Reading football obsessive, but there is something of his need to identify with and hold on to these old heroes in all of us. David Dibben, who reported on Reading's matches for the *Evening Post* for most of the 1970s and shared many journeys to away matches with Downs, is a man with a very different perspective. He showed little interest in discussing the job he did back then, or the personalities and events he had seen, telling me by email, 'I am a person who prefers to look forwards rather than backwards.' Reporting on football matches was a job he did once, and now he was doing other things.

Steve Death was very much in the Dibben camp. For him, being Reading's goalkeeper was a job. Unlike Downs and the ghost players who came to him at Elm Park on the night before the bulldozers arrived, Steve had no wish to revisit past glories or give quotes to passing journalists. For him, once football was done, it was done, and now he was doing something else.

It's ironic that a man who played for 13 years and put himself on the line every week, and who became one of the most popular players to ever play for Reading, did so for a club and a career he held at arm's length. He had no time for nostalgia and focussed only on what was happening now. He had a skill that made him special to thousands but to him was a means of earning a wage and escaping from a conventional life of conforming to the expectations of others. When a journalist knocked on his door to ask him to comment on a former team-mate for an article he was writing, Steve peered through a crack in the door and said, 'I'm not interested.' He had a career full of experiences that most fans could only dream of, and was a hero to thousands, but didn't seem to be as invested in it as the fans to whom he meant so much.

Steve's life was so unlike most people's and yet, in a way, so typical of the rest of us. We drift into jobs, drift out of them, change careers and live out our days while life happens to us. Steve happened to do this while being famous; a strange kind of fame in which he was adored by a few thousand people while remaining virtually unknown to people in the neighbouring county. Glamorous as it seems to the supporter, football was a living for Steve with its rhythms and routines and he was happy to play it to the best of his ability. When the time came to replace those rhythms and routines with those of tending to the greens at Mapledurham, he was equally at ease there, but this time without the attention he had accepted but never sought.

The adulation and publicity came with the territory, but he found it hard to understand why people would be so interested in him. However, he was always happy to sign autographs, was unfailingly polite and would go out of his way to perform acts of kindness without looking for any thanks or praise. David Downs describes Steve as 'introverted but very high-profile.

THE END, AND FINAL THOUGHTS

No one knew him well, but I knew enough of him to know he was a really good guy.'

Unlike most of us, he had a talent that brought genuine pleasure to people who would never know him personally. The recollections of Reading supporters – now, all of us, of a 'certain age' – are a testament to the impact he made on our lives, and the happiness he brought us, simply by being incredibly good at his job. I can still visualise a save he made against Aldershot, diving full length to catch a ball in mid-air that looked as if it was going in the top corner. The game, a 4-0 win, would be forgotten now even by those who played in it, but it lives on for me. Everyone has their own memories, and they make them happy. You can't ask for much more from life than that.

He gave so much to the people of an ordinary town that took him to their hearts, but he gave it by simply doing his job and doing it so well that he was voted as goalkeeper in Reading's imaginary best team some 20 years after his death. Now he finally has a biography written by a fan and with input from team-mates, journalists and other fans. The least I can hope is that he would have appreciated the need for this book, and that he wouldn't have minded too much.

He had an equally powerful and more personal impact on those he played with, as Stuart Morgan told me when he read an early draft of the first chapter, 'Everyone's comments are spot on and it seems like yesterday when I read them. Steve would be so pleased. I've never heard a bad word said about him and he was liked and loved by everyone.'

Richard Wickson remembers meeting Steve's former team-mate Ray Flannigan in 2003, when the ex-goalkeeper was seriously ill, 'I attended a match at Madejski Stadium in 2003 and, knowing I had a connection with the Reading FC Former Players' Association, I was introduced to Ray Flannigan. Ray played for Reading from 1970 to 1972 and played 46 games for the club, scoring his only goal against Bridgwater Town in the FA Cup.

'Ray explained he and his partner were visiting England from their home in Canada and whilst his wife was visiting the Town's Oracle shopping centre, he was taking in a football match. He said he would like to visit the old Elm Park ground and some of his old stomping grounds in Reading before they headed home. So, after the game, I took him up to Norfolk Road to see where Elm Park had once stood. Whilst in the car I informed him that his old team-mate and good friend Steve Death was gravely ill with cancer. Hearing this sad news, he was desperate to see Steve one final time.

'Later on that evening, I arranged with Ray that I would collect him from his hotel on the Caversham Road and take him to see Steve at his home. I agreed that if he knocked on the door and Steve was happy to see him, I would wait for him outside. Steve's wife let him in, and so as not to intrude on the old friends at this intense time I sat in the car awaiting Ray's return.

'After a couple of hours Ray emerged, and it was immediately obvious that he was in tears and greatly distressed, knowing that Steve only had a few days left to live. To see a man that I highly admired in such distress was devastating. Still very upset, I took him back to his hotel and to the arms of his wife. I said my farewells and left.

'Ray died in Canada in October 2015 aged 66, just 12 years after the death of his friend Steve, also from cancer. I will never forget that night and how their friendship meant so much.'

The most important and lasting impact any of us make is on the people we are closest to. I will leave the last words of this book to Alexandria, who deals eloquently with the tensions between fame and privacy, public and private, and her wish to celebrate his memory in the right way. Her comments begin with perhaps the most important thing a child can say about a parent, famous or not, and end with a description of silence, 'He was a great father because I wasn't the easiest child to bring up. He was firm but fair, but he completely understood me.

'I was a bit conflicted when you approached me about this book, but I wanted to put my side across because there have been some things written about my dad that weren't true, including that he left Reading because he had a mental breakdown, which was completely untrue.

'I remember I was approached to ask my dad to give some information on the book about Robin Friday [*The Greatest*

Footballer You Never Saw]. They told me that if I could get him to contribute then I would get to meet the band Oasis. I knew what the answer would be and asked him anyway. He said, "Do you even like the band Oasis?" and I said, "No, not really." So he said, "Then you know what the answer's going to be, don't you?"

'His attitude was that Robin Friday wasn't there to speak for himself, so he didn't want to speak for him. So I was a little bit conflicted because I knew what his attitude was like with the Robin Friday book, but I also wanted to get what he was really like out there.

'I do meet a lot of people, and they say things like "he was such a great goalkeeper" and "if he was only a little bit taller he would have played for England" but at the time when he was playing I never knew all of that. He spoke about his time in digs with Stuart Morgan, but not really about football – it seemed to mostly be about getting drunk.

'I also remember when we were living in Suffolk, he came back to Reading to play in a testimonial for his old team-mate Mark White. He came on and played half of the match and, of course, didn't concede, but I don't think he had anything to do with football apart from that.

'We could stand on the wall at the bottom of the garden and watch him when he was in goal at the Tilehurst End. I knew that he played as a goalkeeper for a living, but I had no idea of how famous he was. I'm not sure he did really, until

THE END, AND FINAL THOUGHTS

when he was very ill in hospital one of the daily papers kept contacting the staff to ask how he was and he wondered why they were interested in him and said he didn't want them to be told anything.

'He was tough but he was squeamish, and he told me that in training once someone was standing on a training bench and fell and had an open fracture of the leg and he said it was the worst thing he'd ever seen. When I was about 25 I had a bike accident and broke and dislocated my wrist. He raced over from Mapledurham to see me, took one look and said, "Oh, my God," and turned and left. I thought, what, is it really that bad?

'He loved horse racing, and we couldn't be in the room if he was watching horse racing. He would have a bet every Saturday, he loved it.

'I still have his last copy of the *Racing Post* that he had with him in the Duchess of Kent Hospice, with all his doodles on it. Doodles are a sign of intelligence because your mind is active all the time. He was very intelligent, but he didn't like doing things because he was expected to, including training!

'They had a match about two days after my dad passed away, and there was a minute's silence. We were with Roy Tranter, one of the club's directors, and he warned us that there would probably be shouting and bad behaviour during the minute's silence, and I wasn't to get upset. I was tense, expecting to hear something, but there was nothing. Afterwards he said that was the best kept silence he had ever seen for anyone.'

Acknowledgements

WHEN I set out to write this book, I wanted it to be a fitting tribute to a great footballer, perhaps the greatest player to have played for my hometown club. I also wanted to safeguard the memory of the Reading team of the 1970s, still considered by many to be the greatest of them all, despite future teams achieving much more in terms of success and playing at the highest level, including three seasons in the Premier League and the highest ever points total in the Football League.

I also wanted the book to be done in the old-fashioned way, with first-hand accounts from people who knew Steve Death, who played with him or watched him from the terraces. As well as this method being my preference, it was also the only feasible way to tell the story of a man who rarely spoke in public and shunned any kind of media exposure. Typing his name into search engines produces some strange and unhelpful results as well and is best avoided.

I would like to take this opportunity to thank all the people who made this book possible, in order of their contribution.

I met **Alan Bunce** after spotting his name as the author of a piece on the public screening of highlights of the 1972 Reading v Arsenal FA Cup tie. Alan kindly offered to meet up one evening and introduced me to **Richard Wickson**. Richard lives and breathes Reading FC and was delighted to be involved. As the founder of the former players' association, he put me in touch with the people I most needed to meet, the players. He also supplied me with facts and figures, and his own memories. Without Richard, this book would not be what it is and would have taken me much longer to write. It would also not have been so much fun, and while researching and writing this book I enjoyed regular catch-ups in Berkshire pubs with Alan and Richard, who I now count as friends.

Alan put me in touch with my first interviewee, **Colin Gunney**, who reported on Reading for the local papers. Colin was also chairman of Steve's testimonial committee and edited the excellent match programme for his testimonial match against a Young England team, managed by Ron Greenwood. I am particularly grateful to Colin for that programme, which is probably the best of its kind I've ever seen, and which gave me much of the information on Steve's early career in schoolboy and youth football in his native Suffolk, as well as detail on his three matches with England Schoolboys.

Colin then suggested I should connect with Steve's daughter **Alexandria**, who he knew was on Facebook. She was generous enough to meet me to share some of her memories of her dad and, later, to 'like' information about the book on social media.

Through Richard Wickson I then met **Stuart Morgan**, who put me in touch with his West Ham colleagues and friends **Harry Redknapp** and **Dave Llewellyn**. Stuart was an old-fashioned centre-half for whom the euphemism 'uncompromising' could have been invented: as a player he was someone you would definitely prefer to play with than against. Add into the mix that he was also an accomplished amateur boxer, and you would expect to be meeting someone quite formidable. He turned out to be a generous, kind and funny person, who couldn't do enough to help me tell his old friend's story. Having been with Steve at both West Ham and Reading, Stuart is uniquely placed to tell that story.

Harry spoke about his memories of the young goalkeeper he saw play for West Ham's youth and reserve sides, and shared stories and memories of Ron Greenwood's coaching and what life was like at the famous West Ham 'academy of football'. Dave spoke warmly about Steve, recalling the early days at Upton Park, and the life of a young apprentice footballer in the late 1960s and early 1970s.

Bobby Williams gave me a long interview, in the hotel foyer of Reading's Madejski Stadium. At 83, Bobby was instantly recognised by a passing supporter and readily posed for a picture with him and broke off for a chat. Bobby's memories were encyclopaedic and would make for a fascinating book in their own right. **Les Chappell**, a personal hero for me as a schoolboy, and **Gordon Cumming** both also shared their experiences, of playing with Steve and also of being a footballer in the 1970s. I didn't tell Les that my sister and I named a pet rabbit after him, and probably shouldn't be admitting it now; I did tell Gordon that I wrote a letter to *Goal* magazine about him in 1972, immediately after he had played out of his skin against Arsenal in the FA Cup.

My thanks also go to **Mark Roach**, presenter of *1871*, the Reading FC podcast, and son of a former club director, for putting me in touch with **Lawrie Sanchez** and **Martin Hicks**. Lawrie was a teenager when he played in the Fourth Division title-winning team of 1978/79, in which Steve broke the Football League record for not conceding a goal. Martin was also in his first full season as a professional in the same season, and later went on to be club captain, as well as overtaking Steve to become the Reading player with the most first-team appearances – a record which still stands today.

Richard then introduced me to **Tommy Youlden**, a key member of the 1975/76 promotion-winning team, playing at centre-half. Tommy had some great insights into playing with Steve, Robin Friday and others as well as some thoughts on the management of Charlie Hurley and the behind-the-scenes workings of the board of directors. **Gary Peters**, a young and virtually ever-present right-back in the 1975/76 team, gave a brilliant analysis of his great goalkeeper and his fellow defenders.

ACKNOWLEDGEMENTS

Tommy put me in touch with **David Downs**, club historian, fan and expert on all things Reading. David was generous with his time and memorabilia including photographs and the detailed scrapbooks he compiled on each season. He also did some fact-checking where there were conflicting versions of key events, drawing on his photographic memory and the excellent archive he has compiled. Having met him a few times, I realised that he would be the perfect person to provide a foreword for the book, and I was delighted that he agreed.

David brokered an introduction to **Graham Nickless**, who reported on Reading during the 1978/79 championship season, and Graham gave me his memories of reporting on that record-breaking campaign.

Wayne Wanklyn described Steve from the point of view of his kindness towards a young apprentice professional, as well as speaking about his own pleasure at being able to do what he had always dreamed of and being a professional footballer with his hometown club. **Mike Kearney**, who played for Reading in two separate spells and has had a long association with the club in a variety of roles, gave me some great insights into playing with Steve for the 1979 champions.

Dave Moreline, who roomed with Steve on away trips and was as close to him as any player, had a fund of stories about his old mate's training – or lack of – and some of the publicity events they had to attend as representatives of the club, while **Paul Bennett** also spent time with me talking about his time as club captain.

Steve Hetzke remembered being a 16-year-old on debut playing in front of Steve and recalled the vastly experienced goalkeeper's consideration for a young player in his very first game as a professional footballer. He also shared his experiences from his nine-year career with Reading. **Mark White** was self-effacing about his own ability – starting with his recollection of scoring an own goal and making another for the opposition – but generous in his praise for his goalkeeper. He also spoke about what it still means to him to have played at this level, and the bonds he still has with his old team-mates.

Reading Chronicle journalists **Roger Ware** and **Alan Porton** also gave me their stories and knowledge from covering Reading for the local papers – a resource that is fast disappearing from the game and that helped bring clubs closer to their communities in the pre-internet age.

Stuart Beavon gave me the perspective of a young player joining the club towards the end of Steve's career and was both funny and revealing about the culture shock of leaving a club in the First Division who had just signed two Argentine World Cup winners and coming to Reading in the Third Division, where things were just a little less professional.

John Turner was fulsome in his praise for Steve's goalkeeping, and shared his fond memories of promotion from the Fourth Division as part of the 1975/76 team, in particular

ACKNOWLEDGEMENTS

the 14 matches he played in the run-in to that season, when he was finally able to get a run in the team at the expense of the regular goalkeeper. John also gave some insights into playing for Brian Clough as a youngster at Derby County.

Neil Webb, who I met through Alexandria Death, had a unique take on Steve, having been a fan on the terraces as a young boy, meeting him as a schoolboy footballer and going on to play with him in the first team at Reading as a 16-year-old. Neil also shared stories about two of the greatest ever managers, Brian Clough and Alex Ferguson, as well as one of Reading's greatest, Maurice Evans.

The last player interview I did was with **Stewart Henderson**, who had a long and distinguished career with Reading, and was coach of the team that won the Fourth Division in 1978/79. Stewart also generously and rather ruefully recounted his role in scoring the own goal that ended Death's famous clean sheet record.

Russell Kempson, a reporter from the *Evening Post*, was my final interviewee for the book, giving me the twin perspective of being a fan watching from the terraces and a journalist conducting a rare and unique interview with Steve – an interview the likes of which will probably never be seen again!

Finally, I would like to thank **Jane Camillin** and the team at **Pitch Publishing**, for immediately saying yes to this project and handling the entire process so professionally. It is a pleasure to work with them. And of course, my thanks to you for buying and reading this book. I hope you enjoyed being transported back to lower-league football in the 1970s, going behind the scenes at an unfashionable club and celebrating a unique character and a great career. Remembering and appreciating the lesser-known and lower-level history of the game is vital to the continued relevance of what is now called the football pyramid. Proponents of super leagues and other abominations of the kind ignore careers and achievements like those of Steve Death and Reading at their peril. Without them, football has no context and little meaning. Thankfully, Pitch Publishing recognises their value and provides a great service to the game as a result.

Afterword

The Making of *Tiny Keeper*

THIS BOOK would not exist in its present form without the help of two people: Alan Bunce and Richard Wickson. Alan was the first person I contacted about the book, having seen his name as the author of a piece on the famous 1972 FA Cup tie against Arsenal. Alan introduced me to Richard and the start of a labour of love began for all three of us. They were so welcoming and so enthusiastic about the book that from our first meeting, I felt as if I was among friends, and their practical support and encouragement has made all the difference. In recognition of their help, and the evenings we spent in pubs around the area, I asked them to share the story of their involvement, in their own words.

Alan Bunce

Getting involved with this book has been a pleasure from the first message I received on LinkedIn from author Alan Hester.

He asked if there was any way I could help. There was some help I could offer, such as a few journalist contacts, but the real help was always going to be from my weekly drinking partner Richard Wickson.

He founded the former players' association and remains friends with players of every era that still survive. Compared to him, mine is something of a supporting role but one that has been a great experience.

What has been most exciting, however, is the thought that I could play a small part in the first book that might let us into the life of Steve Death, someone I idolised as a child, admired as an adult, but who has remained a mystery all that time.

Richard Wickson

Being asked by author Alan Hester was an honour ... and much welcomed.

Since I was retired on medical grounds in 1995, I have been using up my spare time undertaking voluntary work for several organisations. Mostly for my beloved Reading FC.

In 1997, after my medical situation was confirmed, chief executive Nigel Howe gave me many projects to undertake. I started the ball person scheme at Madejski Stadium; I undertook tours of the stadium and, with Grace Kearney, I launched a rebranded Young Royals supporters' club.

In 2000, the then team manager, Alan Pardew, asked me to work with Ron Grant as reserve-team and under-21 kit and equipment manager, which I had the pleasure of doing for over 20 years.

In 1997 I started the Reading FC Former Players' Association which meant contacting, meeting and recruiting all former players and managers that have contributed to at least one first-team appearance – only one ex-player turned my approach down!

That led me to meet many club heroes over the years. In 2017, I resigned from the association to concentrate on my health.

With nothing much to do or keep my mind active, I fell into apathy.

When I was approached by Alan Hester to help him research this book, I was highly delighted. At last, it gave me the opportunity to renew old acquaintances and friendships.

Abiding to legal requirements, I put Alan in touch with past players and members of the club's coaching staff that knew and worked alongside Steve Death.

Who better to shed a light on a man that was an enigma to many. A man that could perform and entertain crowds of between 1,000 and 20,000 every week for over 12 years, but a quiet and unassuming man.

He mesmerised them; inspired them and enjoyed a place in their hearts that would last a lifetime.

Thank you Steve ... and thank you Alan Hester.

Appendix

Steve Death – Reading FC Appearances 1969–82

Season	League	Fa Cup	League Cup	Total
1969/70	28	0	0	28
1970/71	27	4	1	32
1971/72	37	5	1	43
1972/73	46	6	3	55
1973/74	46	2	3	51
1974/75	45	1	6	52
1975/76	32	1	2	35
1976/77	42	3	1	46
1977/78	33	2	0	35
1978/79	46	4	7	57
1979/80	46	4	4	54
1980/81	40	1	4	45
1981/82	3	0	0	3
TOTAL	**471**	**33**	**32**	**536***

*Steve also played in one Watney Cup tie against Manchester United on 1 August 1970.

APPENDIX

Steve was a PFA Divisional Award winner in 1973/74 and 1978/79. He was voted by Reading supporters as the club's player of the season for 1969/70, 1972/73, 1973/74 and 1976/77.